SCIENCE OF ASCENSION

(1929)

A STUDY OF OUR BEING

Contents: Laborless Deliverance; Is Man God; The Science of Our Being; Practical Demonstration; Right Interpretation; Paradise; Roll Away the Stone.

Lillian De Waters

ISBN 1-56459-919-1

Kessinger Publishing's Rare Reprints
Thousands of Scarce and Hard-to-Find Books!

We kindly invite you to view our extensive catalog list at:
http://www.kessinger.net

*To Those Who Would
Know and Practice
Identity*

CONTENTS

CHAPTER		PAGE
I.	Laborless Deliverance	1
II.	Is Man God?	18
III.	The Science of Our Being	49
IV.	Practical Demonstration	73
V.	Right Interpretation	100
VI.	Paradise	129
VII.	Roll Away the Stone	149

PREFACE

BOOKS, Teachers, Instruction, presenting the Kingdom of Heaven within and at hand, are spiritual lamps lighting everyone who presents himself a willing disciple.

Every advancing period delivers a clearer and more practical view of perfect Life and its perfect Expression. As ideas of *God, Self, Universe,* advance to truer conceptions, thought gently rises from the material basis to the true understanding of being.

Absolute Science reveals the truth of individual identity and this Revelation is the Light which "shineth in darkness and the darkness apprehendeth it not."

If one knows not his own identity is it to be wondered that he wanders about as in a dream? How can one demonstrate his perfect immortal identity unless he accepts and understands it?

Absolute Science presents the way of perfect being and perfect universe at hand, and from this point it demonstrates its power, dominion and authority. Waking to the true consciousness of one's being as Spirit, one automatically breaks the yoke of bondage and rises to divine heights.

For those ready and willing to listen and be shown the Science of Ascension, the way is big with blessings. How can one gain a richer and more practical understanding of life except by gaining richer and fuller insight of his own being? "What thou seest, that thou beest," said one with right vision.

Many seem slow to accept advanced ideas and so come to a standstill in understanding and in demonstration. Truth demands that we advance in the spiritual apprehension, understanding and demonstration of Reality as the only fact of existence. The hour strikes for *each* to demonstrate self-knowledge and self-government. The commands of spiritual sense when recognized and fulfilled lead to the illumination of spiritual understanding, restoring the lost sense of one's perfection and revealing *one* God, *one* Christ, *one* Universe, *here and now.*

The glories of revelation await him who, viewing the ascended Christ, accepts this Christ as his own Selfhood.

"Who did hinder you, that ye should not obey the Truth?" (*Gal.* 5:7). Why give power to physical personality, to man-made creeds and laws hindering the glorious sense of individual freedom, power and authority?

Perceiving and obeying the light of impersonal Christ, one makes rapid progress in the practice of Truth and in the overcoming of the false beliefs called sin, sickness and bondage.

Jesus preached Truth, presenting a way of deliverance from suffering and limitation. Spiritual seers since that period have spiritually interpreted his Message, bringing it more clearly to individual and universal recognition and understanding. Truth having been revealed, it needs now to be intelligently understood and practiced.

The significance in which one interprets perfect identity, perfect embodiment and perfect universe determines for him his advancement in individual spiritual demonstration. In proportion as one perceives and accepts the truth that he is Spirit, limit-less, bound-less, law-less, is he prepared to view the glories awaiting his vision.

Learning the power of Soul over sense and Science over belief, we find demonstration easy and natural and this new birth delivers to us ineffable joy, peace and harmony. As sense is uplifted to receive, retain and practice Reality, we are redeemed from erring manifestation and we reach the fruition of the promise: "If ye abide in me, and my words abide in you, ye shall ask what ye will, and it shall be done unto you."

CHAPTER I.

LABORLESS DELIVERANCE

ESUS prophesied that a vision greater than healing the sick, greater even than raising the dead, should some time descend upon us.

Does not vision delivering *cessation* of sin and sickness transcend vision of healing? And would not *immunity* from death transcend raising the dead?

Jesus practiced and taught a Science which enabled him not only to help and bless others on their plane of experience but which lifted himself into a realm or state of consciousness called *ascension*.

Ascension is the door opening to us a new heaven and a new earth. In this perception of

Being we find our immaculate immortality and our transcending glory.

There is a laborless way in which one may leave undesirable earthly conditions. This way is a state of consciousness *wherein such conditions cannot exist.*

If one reports that his body is sick, that his purse is empty, that his mind is sorrowful, the Christ is saying unto him, "The Kingdom of perfect Life is within YOU. In the Kingdom are MANY mansions. Arise! Enter! Behold!"

Here, the notion that one should combat undesirable conditions, or that one should heal undesirable conditions, is laid aside for vision of a higher order. For illustration, let us suppose that upon entering a house one chooses to live in the kitchen. The house has many desirable rooms but in this kitchen he finds himself confronted with dishes, brooms and labor, and he finds that he must deal with them. Thus, his experience becomes unhappy and distasteful.

But why attack brooms and dishes as though they were opposing oneself? Are there not other rooms in which one may live, automatically dispensing with kitchen labor?

One finds instant and tremendous relief in his mind when he perceives that *he need not attack so-called external experience. Rising into a higher realm of thought one automatically transcends undesirable conditions.* As individual consciousness is *uplifted,* conditions simultaneously take on a new aspect. One's whole universe is transformed for him as *he* ascends in consciousness.

We escape the condition called dis-ease as we perceive and understand that WE are immutable Life. We put off limitation and bondage as we accept and practice OUR Reality. Remaining in the library one laborlessly escapes the toils of the kitchen; and entering that realm of consciousness which perceives with Jesus, "*Ye* are the light," one laborlessly puts off darkness.

As the student instructed in music avoids discords by beholding and understanding harmony, so do WE overcome and avoid discordant conditions by beholding and claiming our primitive state of perfect being.

If one considers himself a material being he labors with material limitations. If one considers himself a mental being he labors with mental limitations. But should one cease the belief that he is material, cease also the belief that he is mental, and enter that realm of consciousness wherein he perceives that *he is God-being*, spontaneously he leaves the so-called physical and mental states and enters the state of Spirit.

One finds it utterly impossible to formulate a belief that Spirit can be sick, that Truth can be untrue, that Intelligence can be ignorant. Therefore we open our vision that our King of Glory may appear.

Since we know in our heart that there are no false conditions in Spirit, *then our escape from false conditions is to be Spirit!*

"I say unto thee, Arise," is not spoken to the so-called dead but to the living.

As ignorance is overcome by Intelligence, so human sense is overcome by Spiritual consciousness. The day of attempting to heal so-called *conditions* is drawing to a close. There is being ushered in to view a higher vision,—the *Science of Ascension*; the Science of *being* the Truth; the Science of *spontaneously* experiencing health and blessedness.

With the coming of the automobile the use of the horse began to diminish. With the coming of the radio the use of the victrola lessened. *With the coming of the perception that we are Spirit the conditions called sickness, sin and death begin to vanish.*

Wings are not given a butterfly by the cutting off of feet, nor does one receive heavenly harmony by cutting down or attacking his experience and environment. Not by might but *by spiritual perception*, saith our Lord-Self.

This glorifying Vision—that *we* are the being of Truth, is our new and immortal birth, and in Light such as this *we* perceive our actual being.

Spiritual awakening, or awakening to self as Spirit, is the *up*lifting of individual consciousness into eternal Truth. Perceiving that there is nothing *external* to combat, heal or destroy, one makes rapid strides in individual spiritual advancement; and what is called inharmony, transformed by the higher vision, disappears.

Truth *awakens* us to receive spiritual realities. Truth *calls* us to hear wondrous ideas. With the coming of illumination the DREAM of material existence is dispelled. As light (understanding) appears, darkness (unenlightenment) vanishes. As Christ, our real Self, appears *to us*, un-reality or in-harmony disappears.

"As a vesture shalt Thou change them." . . . "In the twinkling of an eye, we shall be changed."

Thought and vision becoming exalted, no longer does one put new wine into old bottles or patch discordant bodies with right ideas. Wings are not placed upon a caterpillar, nor should one attempt to place a body "white as light" upon a body that is considered mortal and structural.

The immaculate spiritual body (the temple of our Lord), *awaits our claim and our laborless acceptance.* Jesus assured us that his vision reported the perfect universe *at hand,* the white fields *harvested* and the radiant body *prepared.*

'Eye (material vision) hath not seen the things which God hath PREPARED for him." . . . "His going forth is PREPARED as the morning." . . . "Inherit the Kingdom PREPARED for you." . . . "Thou PREPAREST a table before me."

Recognition and acceptance of our God-being enables us to perceive abundance, happiness and harmony, *prepared* and *at hand.* As our immortality becomes apparent to us, the body responds to our ascending vision. Such transfiguration is the *spontaneous* shadowing forth of the new and glorified state of consciousness.

The Science of Ascension, revealing to us that

we are Soul, seizes and holds our vision, and human beliefs and limitations cease proportionately.

Come up higher! This is the call of the One. Come up into a higher perception, and here experience illumination and transfiguration.

"He made darkness his secret place." . . . "The darkness and the light are both alike to Thee."

No matter how great may seem one's mental darkness, there is hidden in him the glory of his Lord. The message that *we are Life, Truth and Love* is the Light that shineth eternally in us though we may comprehend it not. Because of this ever present and transcending Light, one is always delivered, potentially, and no dream ever takes from him his changeless ever present glory and immortality.

Since one is *now* a perfect and immortal being why speak or write at all about redemption, resurrection and ascension? The answer is obvious. If one knew and had demonstrated his redemption, resurrection and ascension he would not be present to ask this question. His body would disappear from material sight and would be deathless.

Jesus Christ presented to us all the way of salvation from false belief,—belief in the reality of material limitation and bondage. Material sense of life must be put off and false belief must yield to Truth, for *"In Christ shall all be made alive."* As one apprehends and retains the correct view of ideal being—perfect, unfallen, changeless identity—the untrue sense of life is *laborlessly* put off and vanquished.

As the Science of Being dawns upon us, we relinquish untrue beliefs for spiritual realization, *establishing in this dream of material existence our understanding of Truth.*

"Ye SHALL KNOW the Truth."—*Jesus.*

We gain the control of Soul over sense in the very way that Jesus taught and demonstrated. In proportion as the truth of Jesus' life and teaching is *apprehended* and *demonstrated* by the individual does the individual "put on," or experience, his harmonious individual identity.

One solves a problem in mathematics understanding that the correct answer already exists, and this perception also applies to the solution of the problem of so-called material existence. The answer is prepared, established from Eternity, and individually one obtains, retains and practices the Science of Being.

"When this mortal shall have put on immortality, then shall be brought to pass the saying that is written, Death is swallowed up in victory."—*Paul*.

True being is not lost, fallen or resurrected, and the Kingdom of eternal harmony remains forever omnipresent in Consciousness. Transition from an *untrue sense* of Life to a *new and true sense* constitutes resurrection.

Being cannot be transformed for the reason that being is changeless and *im*mortal. It is wrong *belief* or mistaken *sense* which must yield to the harmony of spiritual sense or to the Science of Ascension.

Although individual spiritual identity is actually immortal, perfect and complete, and not imperfect, human and mortal, nevertheless the *perception* of this fact seems to dawn upon one by degrees. Spiritual understanding is perceived and demonstrated by the individual gradually and gently, culminating in the divine requirement: *"Be ye therefore perfect."*

Our individual demonstration of Spiritual Power over false sense becomes evident only as we rise to our nativity in Spirit. One emerges step by step from the belief that he is material and mortal to the recognition that he is Spirit and that all his experience is spiritual. A metaphysical teacher wrote: *"Emerge gently from matter into Spirit."*

We wait expectantly and finally the child disappears and the man takes his place; yet the man is always here potentially and actually. We discern and perceive Truth spiritually and finally the unreal (sense) disappears and the real state is enthroned. Perfect being is always here inherently and eternally.

With the disappearance of the caterpillar the crawling motion is gone automatically. The butterfly does not crawl. With the disappearance of the mortal (untrue belief), the sick and dying habits are gone. Immortal being is not sick or sinful. With the acceptance in individual consciousness of the perfect changeless state the untrue expression ceases *automatically*.

"*Overcome evil with good.*" Overcome the belief of mortality with the realization of Immortality. Overcome the belief of sick, discordant body with the conviction of perfect and changeless body. Overcome the unawakened state of consciousness with the living fire of insight and perception.

"The law of the Spirit of life in Christ Jesus hath made me free from the law of sin and death."—*Paul*.

IMMORTAL being is not bound by fetters or hampered by dreams. Immortal being is free Spirit, omnipresent, omniscient and omnipotent. Let this be our vision.

The putting on of immortality is the AWAKENING *to the fact that a spiritual being is perfect and that there is no other being!*

Nothing opposed to Reality can ever actually exist. Opposition and separation appear only to dull eyes and dim vision. Perfect being never changes, no matter what may be one's view-point. As the individual harmonizes his vision with Reality he *laborlessly* experiences peace, power, glory and immortality.

"*The light shineth* IN *darkness and the darkness comprehendeth it not.*"—*John.*

As the light shineth IN darkness so health shineth in one who reports sickness; and IN him who declares that two and two are five there still abides consciousness of the fact that two and two are four. Thus our infinite Self supplies all our needs, fulfills all our desires and delivers all our ideals.

Truth, true and ideal being, is here without beginning and without ending. *Individual sense, however, perceives, accepts and demonstrates the full dominion of Spirit according to individual faith, vision and understanding.*

One's life is not here in a coming state, but his life is here in a perfect and complete state. The same thing may be said of individual embodiment. It rests with us each to perceive and demonstrate this eternal fact of Being.

"Be ye reconciled to God" is Scriptural advice. Let us reconcile ourselves to the fact that we are dealing with one Substance only. Vision such as this quickly clears away the cloud, quickens the faith and brings one *face to face* with his reality.

Jesus showed us the pathway leading from the state called mortality (human sense) to the actual state of immortality (Spirit). He portrayed to us, how the dream of material existence may be broken, how dream laws may be set aside, and how sickness, disease, sin and death may be *laborlessly* annihilated.

It has been scientifically stated that either by suffering or by Science one comes to himself,—one arrives at the point *"Be ye therefore perfect."*

"YE SHALL KNOW the Truth," declared Jesus. We are not required to "know the Truth" *after* we have regained our perfect state (returned to our Father's home), but *now, in the dream of material existence, is the time and place for us to discern and experience the Truth that delivers us to freedom.*

This Truth may become known to us individually, either through suffering,—the overcoming, *step by step*, of false sense with true ideas,—or, through Science of Ascension.

There is a Way *above* the taking of human steps, above suffering, above climbing and laboring. This way is the Science of Ascension, the Science of Fulfillment, the Science of "The last shall be first," the Science of "Fields white already to harvest."

In our every day experience we see ways of traveling from one geographical place to another. One may walk over the distance, he may motor or he may travel by aeroplane. But if he could bridge that distance by *being there* without any process of traveling or "going," this deliverance would illustrate the Science of Ascension.

The Prodigal son was confronted with the problem of regaining his perfect state of being. So are we. If in the attempt to return one takes the mental position of climbing, overcoming, laboring, this process is what has been termed the way of "suffering"; for here one is supposed to learn Truth through experience, and this entails constant effort, practice and labor.

If, however, one glimpses the fact that he has

never left his perfect Kingdom, then he sees that he is not required to return; he is required only to know that he has never wandered away but in a dream, and that he is now and here, uninterruptedly and unchangingly, a perfect being of Life, Truth and Love.

This is *laborless deliverance.* This is not the Science of moving up and on but the Science of *remaining still;* not the Science of putting on or putting off experience but the Science of *recognizing and accepting Reality.*

The Science of Ascension is the Science of *laborless deliverance,* the Science of seeing *face to face,* the Science of *experiencing* Reality.

CHAPTER II.

Is Man God?

TO announce that *we are Spirit* means that we recognize and accept Spirit, God, as our reality and as our true Self.

Many have refrained from accepting the wonderful vision that *we are Life, Truth and Love*, because of the boldness of the statement; but when this fact is stated in another way, when it is couched in different phraseology, one readily confirms and sanctions it.

Let us be big enough in vision and great enough in nature to recognize and accept truth no matter who states it or in what raiment of words it be clothed. One of insight penetrates the garment of language and knows that the leaven is working no matter how many measures of meal may seem to conceal it.

Suppose we are asked the current, metaphysical query, *"Is man God?"* What is our reply?

Our reply is this. The question cannot be intelligently answered, as it stands, for the reason that the words *"God"* and *"man"* are opened to many different interpretations. But if one pierces the wall of ambiguity and discerning the underlying meaning, asks the question in more precise language, it can be satisfactorily answered.

Let the question be stated: *"Are we Life, Truth and Love?"* This language is understood and does not need interpretation as though it were a foreign tongue.

When one hears the word *man*, immediately the mind questions, "Does this mean the real or the false man? Does this question refer to the mentality, the Soul, or the body?" If therefore, students, teachers and writers avoid using the word *man* and substitute a word which is common and easily understood, much confusion occurring in metaphysical teaching will be eliminated.

The same misunderstanding occurs with the word *God*. Here one, spiritually unenlightened, may regard "God" in a personal sense. We therefore, use the words Truth, Spirit, Soul, Reality, etc., to bring the light more clearly to individual consciousness.

Writers of the Bible, as well as some well-known metaphysical writers of recent times, speak of "man" as *image, expression, manifestation, idea*. Can it be that this image means *you* and *me*—the *individual, himself?* Can it be that I, myself, am an image, an expression, a manifestation only?

Verily, no. There is no one but whom as soon as he receives a certain baptism of the fire of insight, chafes under the notion that he, himself, is an "image." There is something in him which whispers to him that he is *greater* than an image, *greater* than a manifestation or an idea. If he penetrates a little more deeply, if he opens his vision a little more fully, he soon perceives just *what* it is that is the image and just what it is that is called *man—the image of God.*

It is the body that is the image. The body is the manifestation or expression of individual consciousness. The body *images, enacts, portrays, expresses, manifests* the health, life, strength, power, intelligence, substance and reality of individual consciousness.

Perceiving that *man is the body* or *embodiment* one can then clearly accept that God (invisible Life) is not man (visible body) nor is man (visible body) God,—YET THEY ARE ONE AND INSEPARABLE.

One would not say that the person outside the mirror is the form *in* the mirror. The person outside is not an image or expression, but the form in the mirror is the expression of that form standing before the mirror. One is not the other, still they are ONE and they are INSEPARABLE.

Thus if one questions, *Is man God?* the answer is: "Man, or image, is not God, or Substance; but they are one as Intelligence and idea; Manifestor and manifestation; Soul and embodiment.

Individual body (man or manifestation) is the activity, expression and manifestation of individual Self.

We do not consider Self a picture or an idea or a manifestation. Such belief would not agree and coincide with our living Teacher, who says throughout all ages, times and discoveries, "I AM THE LIFE, I AM THE TRUTH, I AM THE WAY!"

Individual being, or the *being* of the individual, is the one Life, Intelligence and Substance. There is only ONE being and this one is ALL. We cannot have being outside this ONE. *All* being is Christ, God. *All life* is Reality, God. *All* intelligence is Truth, God.

Have no fear in stepping out upon the waves

of new ideas and in claiming the glory of your immaculate being. Individual being comprises *both* consciousness and body, both Life and its expression, *for they are one and inseparable.* To consider oneself manifestation *only,* is to fear to step out upon the great sea of understanding.

Everything that is real, that is true, that is perfect is included in the One. The One is Universal (Father) and individual (Son)—*one* being. *The reality of the individual Self can be nothing else than the one Reality, for there is nothing else to be.*

One can easily perceive that all nature symbolizes that the son is a son for a time until finally he "puts on," or becomes, a father. In the beginning of our metaphysical study, we would no doubt have been startled had we been informed the majesty and the omnipotence of our being. However, we found it easy to be children of God, sons and daughters of God, manifestations and ideas of God. But hearts now leap to the music of the fuller vision, and exaltedly one receives the new name in his forehead.

How could Intelligence and its idea be divided? How could Soul and its embodiment be separated? Nay, it cannot be. Life, Being, is one, and this one is *all inclusive*. The universe, including man (body of the individual), is the body of Truth, God.

"Thine eyes did see my substance, and all my members were fashioned when as yet there were none of them."—*David*.

The real body, the perfect body, the divine body, is the man-ifestation of Wisdom, Intelligence, Life, Substance, Being, *and it is this perfect, immaculate body that is called man—the image of God.*

Let us claim the highest, so shall the Highest claim us. It has been said by men of wisdom that as one approaches Truth so does Truth approach him. If one feels that he must not hope for or expect too much, that it might be safer to be son than Father, let him consider such Scriptural advice as this.

"Let us come *boldly* to the throne of grace.... Great is thy *boldness* of speech.... *Ye* are the light of the world.... Let *your* light shine.... Fear not! No man may say that Jesus is the Lord, but by the Holy Ghost."

Thus, we are both Creator and creation; both Intelligence and idea; both Soul and body. And this unit is *indivisible, inseparable, irresistible, everlasting* and *eternal*.

It is curious that an understanding of the *body* is one of the last revelations to come to many, yet one of the first questions that a student asks. The thought of the body seems often to tear one asunder.

Now many of us have discovered that we do not understand a thing until we are in a position to understand it. That is, we may hear or read a right answer to a question, yet our ears and eyes are dull and blinded and often the meaning escapes us. Years later, perhaps, the right answer presents itself again, and now how differently it appears to us. We hail it with great joy. The answer is always here, but one perceives Truth according to his individual receptivity.

When one takes ownership of his body, *as though his body were outside his consciousness,* he feels a responsibility and very often a heavy one. If, for instance, the body seems weak and sick, his belief may be that it should be fixed up so that it will look right and act right again. By assuming personal ownership over his body, he automatically assumes responsibility and makes himself *personally* accountable for the health, harmony and maintenance of his body. Is this not so?

Shall we then stop feeding the body, clothing the body, caring for the body? Not at all. *But we can change our perception of body.* We can come into a higher understanding of body and automatically bless not only our bodies and ourselves, but bless the whole world.

Yea, Self does not have a body of destructible flesh and bones—a body subject to age, limitation and disease. Do you suppose that a *Spiritual* being could be weak and weary, old and crippled? Unthinkable!

Do you recall how Jesus brought attention to the growing of the lily? How beautiful its body! How fragrant its perfume! How irresistible its form! Yet how wholly *unconscious* of its body. Jesus, discerning our need said, Consider the lily. It assumes no responsibility. yet behold its beauty of form and its radiance of being. And you, do you not know that infinite Reason places you in a far higher position than this lily growing in the field? Is it not to be expected that *you* have a form and a body superior to that of a simple flower growing in the earth?

Sitting under a great shade-tree one day, listening to the carol of the birds and the hum of the bees, it came to a thoughtful person how much more he would enjoy nature at that moment were he not fatigued. There seemed a sense of unrest in his body. Quite naturally he carried on a conversation with his inner self about it.

"Life would be so much more delightful," he meditated, "if people were never sick, if the body were not subject to disasters, discords, limitations. Of course, there isn't really any such body but there seems——"

"Well, why should you think about your body?" came back the answer.

"Yes," he thought, "that's it. Why should I be *compelled* to think of it? I really know so little about the body anyhow. I do not understand how I live nor how I sleep in the body. I do not understand how my blood circulates nor how my food digests. In fact, now that I see it, I know little or nothing about the body as far as the substance or the reality of it is concerned."

"Well then, why have *any* unnecessary care or worry over it at all? Can there be any body except the body of Truth? Is there anything *besides* Truth?" questioned the Voice.

"What a wonderful thought!" he mused. "To be sure, Truth is my consciousness, and why shouldn't Truth be my body as well? Am I consciousness *and* body?"

"You are not dual," came the answer. "You are one. Whatever there is of you must be the ALL of you. You are Myself. I am Yourself. Your body is Mine. My body is yours. This is one Whole, one ALL, one Being, one action, one form, one Life and one embodiment of this Life."

Unconsciously he had been caught up by Spirit, and now simultaneously there came to him an illumined sense of joy, uplift and harmony.

Have we not all noticed that when the body is perfectly well and normal that it causes us no concern,—in fact, we quite forget it for the time? We have it, of course, but it is much the same as a shadow; it goes along with us wherever we wish to go, but we have no anxious concern about it, and at times we are altogether unconscious of it.

Turn now to a consideration of the night dream. You dream, for instance, that you are traveling with a party of friends in an ocean liner. You plainly see the great ship; you watch the white waves; you look upon your friends and you distinguish them; you see the color of their hair and eyes and you note their mode of apparel. But you do all this unconsciously, that is, with no conscious thought as to whether they are material, mental or spiritual beings.

If you wish, you could gaze into the mirror at your side and see your own reflection. A body to be sure,—hair, eyes, hands and feet, also apparel. You run down the stairs, but you do not give your feet a thought. You sit at a table and perhaps dine sumptuously yet it does not occur to you that you have a stomach, and certainly you have not heard of indigestion. You dance upon the polished floor and your joy and abandon are glorious. You are not considering whether or not your body is weary; you are not considering your body at all.

Should you feel impelled to sing to your friends, you give no thought as to whether or not your voice has been cultivated. It does not occur to you that you have a throat, yet, laborlessly, wonderful tones now come forth, and words, too. But you quite take this for granted.

Now, you see that in your dreams you have hands and feet and body; you walk and run and sing and dance; you talk and play and eat. Although you are unconscious of a body yet it accompanies you. Is this not so?

Turning now to this world, is it not easy to acknowledge that you perform many necessary and important acts relative to living, yet such action is quite unconscious on your part, and quite laborless too? You waken in the morning, for instance, but you do not know how this is done.

You are quite unconcerned, however, as you have been doing this laborlessly for days, months and years. It passes your attention unnoticed.

You partake of breakfast, yet you attend not to the digestion of this food or to the operations through which it passes in order to nourish the body. At night you "go to sleep" but you have never yet discovered just how you do this little thing. Indeed, if you tried to investigate it, you might be unable to accomplish it.

When your body is radiant with the glow and glory of perfect health you quite forget about it. The more health, the less thought of body; full health, no thought of body at all. Now this by no means infers that we are bodiless, but it means that our body has no *personal* claim upon us. We should feel no responsibility regarding the body and we should feel no attachment to it.

Has the hour struck for us when we are willing to be "absent from the body and present with the Lord"? Are we ready to yield attachment and responsibility that a personal sense of body brings? Are we not told in mystical language that it is in "losing" that one gains? Have no fear that in losing *attachment* to the body, you may lose the body itself, for quite to the contrary, you will be fitting yourself to understand it.

Oh, wondrous, radiant light! Oh, glorious, ever-increasing revelation! To be willing not to heal or change the body is to find oneself on the royal road to a body that is not sick, limited or changeable,—a body immortal, eternal and everlasting. *A body immune.*

It has been said that everything is as real as one makes it. Now no one makes Reality for reality IS, regardless of what anyone thinks or believes or feels. If one believes that his body is material, if a material body is reality to him, then automatically he subjects his body to so-called material action. But supposing one lays no claim to a separate, external or personal body at all, would not he then be out of the touch of disease, limitation, destruction, altogether?

Consider this momentous question slowly, meditatively. Finding the true idea of a thing, the false idea drops away *automatically*. Bearing this in mind, it would seem wisdom that we perceive WHY our bodies cannot be sick; then we will be fearless and immune. The time is here for each of us to see that we have no false body to deny, and that all form belongs to the one Life and Being.

Truth is not in any form but Truth is every form. Being is not divided into form but being is expressed by form. We cannot go out of life for we ARE life. We cannot go out of health for life IS health. We cannot be outside the Kingdom, for the Kingdom is WITHIN us. We cannot be separated from body for body is *one with Soul*. We *cannot* be separated, divided, disunited. *We are complete and indivisible being.*

Since Reality is all, and all is Reality, then

whatever the body is, it must be in and of Reality. Clear vision reports that Soul and body, Cause and effect, Life and form are ONE, *now, always and forever.*

When we go to the telephone and listen to a friend's voice, we know that back of the instrument is the man himself, and the instrument is but the form or the medium of transmission. Now it is quite the same with Soul and body, with Creator and creation. Form is the medium of expression, form is as necessary and as eternal and indestructible as is the Self which it is expressing. Perfect embodiment is the body of Truth. Spirit blessed the form called *creation* and called this formation *good, perfect* and *ideal.*

Do not worry about the teaching of reincarnation, which means the changing of forms; nor of pantheism, which means the placing of Spirit *in* creation. Soul is limitless, infinite, eternal; in everything and yet in nothing. Neither here nor there, yet everywhere. Neither this one nor that one, but everyone. The One shining in the star, sparkling in the water, blooming in the rose, ascending in the bird, seeing, hearing, feeling, expressing in all life and being.

Truth in the small, Truth in the great; Truth in heaven, Truth in earth. One Being, one all. The One, all height and no height; The One, all time and no time; the One, all form and no form; the One all language and no language; the One all motion and no motion; the One *indescribable, unspeakable, incomparable!*

The One says: You are my infinite Self. All that I am, you are. All that is Mine is also thine. You are immortal being including immortal form. Your form is My idea made visible. You are not something that has Soul; you ARE Soul. Being is not something that has body; being *includes* body. As Soul is eternal so also is body eternal. Body, form, is the expression of perfect living Self-existence.

Our Father Being, Hallowed be Our name,
Our Kingdom is come. Our will is being done
On earth as it is in Heaven.
We give this day of our daily bread.
We joyously forgive all debts and debtors,
We are not led into temptation
But we are delivered from all evil,
For Thine, Mine, *Ours* is the Kingdom,
The power and the Glory for ever.

Insight alone can sharpen the eye to function to fourth dimensional vision and to right interpretation of a spiritual universe.

Fourth dimensional sight is that sight which is able to see in the dark ("the light shineth *in* darkness"); which reports order instead of disorder; harmony instead of discord; unity instead of division.

Looking toward the self-existent Heights, great Seers have boldly proclaimed that evil has no existence whatever. Such vision swallows up duality as light takes up shadow.

Those of us visioning toward the City which lieth four-square, find it helpful to pore over in our minds words attuned to a higher order.

words yielding nourishment to the mind like rain to the parched ground.

Let us inbreathe and breathe out such words as *infinity, eternity, freedom, victory, triumph, omniscience, omnipresence, omnipotence, almighty, everlasting, ascension.*

Let the cares and worries of false sense go, and vision the presence of Reality. Let the reports of mind and body go and hear the voice of Christ.

Illusion is not in the thing itself. Illusion is in the false concept of that thing. Interpreting creation through the veils of time, space and personality, is it any wonder that one reports division, duality, relativity?

Light is light, not darkness nor twilight. A circle is a circle, not a square of a cube. Two and two are four, not three or five. And so "perfect Creation" as pictured in the beginning (Genesis), and in the end (Revelation), is without spot or blemish, pure as crystal, scintillating as the most precious stone, radiantly reflective as the clearest mirror.

This brings to my remembrance a particular moment in which my mind swiftly and clearly functioned to ever present reality, despite the hearing of a false report.

I was wakened in the middle of a night's rest by the telephone. The report came that some one was suddenly ill, that an organ of the body was functioning very improperly. Coming out from a sound sleep, I said the first thing that came from my consciousness. "Tell him that two and two are four."

The person to whom I spoke thought that I was still sleeping, or only partly awake, and refusing to accept my message tried to induce me to send him a *spiritual* message, something that would be appropriate to his condition.

But I was adamant. That was what I saw and that was my message. *Tell him that two and two are four!* That was final. That was all.

The following morning that man himself came to see me. He looked perfectly well and he said he was perfectly well. "But what a queer message you sent me," he objected.

"Did you not find that you went immediately to sleep that your 'attack' vanished?"

"Yes," he admitted. "That is true but——"

"I will interpret that message for you," I said, "for the interpretation is the reality that healed you. I knew that *you* could not change life nor its natural functions. The message that two and two are four means *Life is Life*. Life is not sickness, pain and falsity. Life is perfect, changeless, glorious being. Truth is that which IS, and *you* can't change it. *You are reality for there is nothing else for you to be.*"

This illustrates clearly that it is the *spontaneous treatment* which delivers,—the treatment that leaps over words, that transcends dimensions, that standing alone declares a thing to be so because it is. That does not say; I will dress it in this gown or clothe it in these phrases so that it will be appropriate for the illusion, but boldly and with authority, Truth speaks from the heart; speaks from that blaze of glory which transcends dreams and dream language.

One should never hesitate to speak from his illumined state of consciousness at that precise moment, for then one is the Fire which consumes and the Power which delivers.

Life is not something that one may choose to believe, but life is what it is, despite anyone's belief about it. Perfect individual life, perfect functioning of that life, perfect glory and immortality of that life is independent of anyone's belief or thought about it. Let us therefore apprehend Life as it is, praise it as it is, express it as it is.

Perfect law of Spirit neither obeys nor disobeys mental and physical law. It is a law unto itself. It is the Self-existent and only. Its command is, *Let there be light! Let it come forth!*

Recognizing oneness in consciousness, the dove of Peace again descends and power is given to function to the Christ mind. But some may continue with material and mental methods of help and healing until they are ready for the higher position.

Our being is actually three-fold,—Father, Son and Holy Ghost. In my textbook, *The One,* there is given a clear and scientific presentation of our Trinity in unity.

Should one read wonderful statements of Truth, absorbing these with eyes and ears only, not perceiving anything fresh or new about them but interpreting them through former belief and conviction, he receives no revelation of Truth, no inspiration or illumination.

But, if as one reads, there comes forth a quick response from within him like the moving of a living thing,—something warm, vital, uplifting like the blazing up of a living fire—this is revelation. One is then actively drinking of the River of the Water of Life.

Since our being is three-fold, how do we interpret the Father or first position of our trinity? Since "No man hath seen the Father at anytime," the Father is the UNSEEN presence. The *Father* of us is our unseen Life, Intelligence, Substance and Reality. The Father is our irresistible Actuality, our changeless Being, our I AM.

Having meditated upon this first position and accepted it, one next takes up the *Son*. Who is the Son? Since the Father is the invisible Life, Truth, Being, Reality,—who can the Son be?

The Son is Emmanuel, or God with us. The Son is therefore the Invisible *expressed*. The Son is Consciousness *individualized*,—the individual being, the individual identity.

We are *both* the Father and the Son, *both* the Universal and the individual, and they are ONE, *inseparable and indivisible*.

We could not be the Father, Universal, without being also the Son, individual. The Father would be unidentified without the Son (individual identity), and the Son would have no being without the Father (Universal Substance).

The Holy Ghost is *Self*-illumination, *Self*-consciousness and Understanding *embodied*. To illustrate. We walk down the avenue and see a man carrying a sign "I am blind." How can the Father, Son and Holy Ghost be here? Well, the man is alive, and he would not be alive without *life*. This unseen life is *God the Father*.

He has individuality, he says "I", and this individual identity is *God the Son*.

Now why does he appear blind? Because of the veil of ignorance. He is not *consciously* aware of his spiritual identity. The fire in him has not been kindled. Although he is the sight of God he acts like a blind man. But supposing that it came to him, or he heard, that he is a divine being, that his power to see is God and thus he *cannot* be separated from his perfect sight.

Day by day it is with him. He sleeps with it, he eats with it, he continually feels, *I am a divine being, I am a perfect being, I am a God-being.* Finally, this truth comes to absorb his mind *completely.* Then comes the blaze, then shines the glory. Illumination, inspiration leaps up within him and his sight is *re-stored.*

Now this spiritual influx of light and glory which he has experienced, is the *Holy Ghost,* and it is in this Light that he sees himself, that he finds his body manifesting his glory and his per-spection. The coming of the Holy Ghost heralds the "healing."

The coming of the Holy Ghost is the *absorbing of false beliefs, the rising into new joys, the showing forth of a body free from delusion.*

"And Jesus said, What I have done, all men will do; and what I am all men will be."—*Aquarian Gospel.*
"And his name shall be called The Mighty God, the Everlasting Father."—*Isaiah.*

The notion that individual being is an image impedes individual spiritual advancement. Our individuality is the *one* Life, Truth and Love. This Life, Truth and Love was individualized, seen and interpreted as *Jesus Christ;* and this same Trinity-in-unity is individualized in you and in me. *Am I claiming it?* This each must answer for himself.

He advances most in understanding and demonstration who not only sees the heights but aspires to the knowledge of Jesus Christ, individualizing infinite power and *demonstrating* the *kingdom* of heaven in his midst.

The perception that *we* are the Trinity, that individual being is Being individualized, delivers to us a fearless wing and mighty victory. Vision such as this, accompanied with fire of insight and courage of conviction, *demonstrates* the might of Omnipotence to the "*pulling down of strong holds, the casting down imaginations and every high thing that exalteth itself against the knowledge of God.*" (2 Cor. 10:4-5).

Let us not be content with the letter of the

Word, no matter how attractively we express it; nor how earnestly we listen to it. Let us aspire for *the spirit of the Word!* Of what avail are scientific words unaccompanied by *"fire in the mouth"?* Of what advantage is a fire-place stacked with logs when no match is provided?

Yea, the resplendent flame of Spirit, in the twinkling of an eye, consumes the false images of human thought, burns the chaff of erring belief, and lo, here stands individual spiritual being—the Christ,—clothed in the Mind of Omnipotence.

"Behold, I will make my words in thy mouth fire."—(Jer. 5:14).

As we need both the match and the logs in order to obtain heat, so both the letter (understanding) and the Spirit (fire in the mouth) are demanded of us that we may put on our robe of Glory and receive His name in our forehead.

CHAPTER III.

THE SCIENCE OF OUR BEING

ABOUT half a century ago, a noted writer of Metaphysical Science stated in her text-book:

"That we are Spirit and Spirit is God is undeniably true. . . . The final understanding that we are Spirit must come. . . . At present we know not what we are, but this is certain, that we *shall be* Love, Life and Truth when we understand them."

Has not the belief that we are human beings, subject to errors of the flesh, resulted in the limitation and discord enacted upon the face of the earth today? And will not the understanding that we are Soul, Spirit,—the recognition and acceptance of the actuality of our being—be the Truth that shall set us free from this false belief?

By identifying self as Life, Soul, one *automatically* rises to new heights.

"I, if I be lifted up, will draw all men unto me," spoke Jesus Christ. As peerless Christ Truth is lifted before our vision, recognition and understanding take place and our whole universe reflects this glory.

"Ye *must be born again*" was Jesus' testimony. The act of yielding up untrue beliefs for true understanding constitutes this rebirth.

Was it not because Jesus claimed and acted his *deity* that he infuriated the Jews? "This man," thought they, "who wears clothes, who eats and drinks and sleeps exactly the same as we do, claiming that he is God,—claiming that he is different from us. We are human and he is human."

And so they said to Jesus: "For a good work we stone thee not; but for blasphemy; and *because that thou, being a man, makest thyself God!*"—(*John* 10:33).

They had insight enough to see that Jesus individualized Almighty power in healing the sick and in raising the dead, but their ignorance and human sense kept them from perceiving that Jesus not only claimed this almighty Authority for himself but that he claimed it for *everyone*.

Jesus was the ideal Self. He was God in the flesh. And whatever is true of Jesus is likewise true of us all. No wonder we love to talk about Jesus. His great love for mankind prompted him to demonstrate to the very end his absolute Understanding of unchangeable life and being,— to portray to the whole universe that he had the keys to heaven.

> "I love to tell the story
> Of unseen things above;
> Of Jesus and his glory,
> Of Jesus and his love."

Can we perceive that *we* are Life, Truth and Love except we first perceive that *Jesus was Life, Truth and Love? We cannot.*

"No man cometh unto the Father but by me." "Other foundation can no man lay than Jesus Christ." . . . "He that acknowledgeth the Son hath the Father also."

The study of the life of Jesus touches our hearts, wakens our love, and as WE identify Self as Christ, we identify Self as life, truth, glory and power.

Whatever Jesus claimed for himself he claimed also for US. Hear his vibrant, startling words: *"That they* ALL *may be one in us. . . And the glory which Thou gavest me, I have given* THEM. *. . That* THEY *may be made perfect in one."*

The Christ (true belief) of you says: "I am the Life, I am the Truth, I am the Father, I am God." The human (untrue sense) says: "I am in limitation, I am in prison, I am in bondage."

Shall we identify ourselves as limited, human being, or shall we identify ourselves as free- flawless, triumphant Christ? Let 'Absolute Science decide for us. Absolute Science is the Science of high Vision, ascending from glory to glory.

A great vision of Reality now sweeps over the world. Soon it will be more universally perceived and accepted that life is not a problem for the individual to solve. Its solution has already been reached. It remains now for the individual to *accept* the solution and *experience* the glory.

It is not that our health, for instance, is coming to us, but rather is it that our health is HERE. According to individual recognition of this fact does this health *appear*. It is not that the Kingdom of heaven is coming to us, nor is it that earth is evolving into heaven, but the fact for our attention is that *perfection is here—reality is at hand*.

How much of heaven are we perceiving? *As much as our individual state of consciousness permits.*

"*Agree with thine adversary quickly,*" directed Jesus. Reach a positive position of agreement and perception. "*Nothing shall by any means hurt you,*" continued he who knew. We do not shoulder a gun and go forth into an external universe to attack our enemy, but right where we are, we stand still and *behold* our salvation. We acknowledge it. We accept it.

We believe that because Spirit is all and is infinite that WE are this infinity. How could it be otherwise? Since Reality cannot be separated or divided, WE are this Reality. It is easy enough to believe that God-Self cannot lack; God-Self cannot be afraid; God-Self cannot be limited; God-Self cannot be destroyed.

It is said that the one of vision sees nothing but good, just as "to the pure all things are pure." The one of vision sees goodness, not as the opposite of evil (un-good), but he sees goodness as *omnipresence*.

The same with health. One of vision does not see health as the opposite of sickness, but he sees health as wholeness and as everpresence. One of Insight reports according to the vision of Reality.

Preach deliverance to those who are held captive by matter and mind (untrue belief)! As light kindles light so recognition and praise of the Jesus Christ Self bring forth radiance and glory of mind that CANNOT be deceived: of body that CANNOT be sick; of being which is verily Christ.

When thought is raised to the true state of being—the sense of Spirit—it is the mind of Christ.

Jesus brought to this world a way out of ignorance. He showed a path which was neither warfare nor separation, but on the contrary, was *at-one-ment, oneness* and *unity.* Jesus' vision was to "agree." *Yea, he, himself was this at-one-ment or agreement.*

Had Jesus come into this world clothed in the body of ascension, he would not have been seen here; but "He took upon himself the form of a servant, and was made in the likeness of men" that he might be visible to those in this state of consciousness. From position of oneness with us he showed us his *actual* state of being, *our* actual and perfect state of being.

Jesus himself was our Way. He unified, he blessed, he forgave, he fulfilled, he agreed and he redeemed.

Did Lazarus come forth as a living being because Jesus called him? No. It was because he *was* a living being that Jesus called him.

Was it because of lack of food that Jesus supplied baskets full of bread and fish? No. It was because of ABUNDANCE of food that Jesus did this very thing.

Was it because the man's arm was withered and lifeless that Jesus told him to stretch it forth? No. It was because his arm was perfect and changeless that Jesus commanded, STRETCH IT FORTH!

Was it because Jesus was functioning to opposites that he walked triumphantly upon the waves, passed invisible through the multitude, commanded the sick to be as the well, perceived the "sinning woman" as sinless, and the so-called dead as the living?

It was because Jesus functioned in unity, in indivisibility, in oneness, in his Kingdom HERE and on earth NOW that he enacted this power.

Jesus' advice was to *leave the so-called external world alone.* I walk in it, he said, but I am not of it; I am not affected by it. I eat the food from the table, true, but I have other food as well. I live and eat and walk in your world, apparently, but TO MYSELF I am living and eating and walking in a world that you do not, as yet, comprehend. This world is the world I have told you about—The Kingdom of Soul.

Jesus did not present any outer way of atonement, but he did show us an *inner* way, a spiritual recognition that is to take place *within individual* consciousness.

The following steps are to be taken by the individual as he rises from sense to Soul, individually ascending the ladder of life.

FIRST: Recognition that the so-called external universe is not external but is picturization, or expression of thought and vision.

SECOND: Recognition that the belief in so-called evil indicates a lack of individual consciousness of the understanding of fulness, oneness, completeness and unity.

THIRD: The final state is the immersion of individual sense into full, clear vision of Reality. The individual has now accomplished his at-onement and is resurrected into the "new man," the Christ-Self, the God-being who, ascending above all earthly beliefs, functions in Reality.

We read in Genesis, "*And God saw everything that he had made, and, behold, it was very good.*" The perfect Creator and perfect Creation here mentioned, portrays infinite Spirit and its infinite manifestation as All-in-all. All life is pronounced immortal, changeless, eternal, and all manifestation perfect and good.

Now Genesis in continuing, mentions a *second* creation appearing after the first. What can this second creation be except an untrue interpretation of the first? Or the first perfect and complete Creation seen materially instead of spiritually; seen imperfectly and incompletely instead of seen perfectly and completely; seen darkly as through a glass instead of seen clearly *face to face?*

A Spiritual, individual being shall "know the Truth," shall know his power, his might, his dominion, his joy, his peace, his wonder, his eternity, his infinity, his wholeness and his invariableness.

Therefore, we behold right here and now the actual truth of Creator and Creation. Moses speaks of the second creation as a (mental) "mist," and Paul calls it a "riddle," while St. John (of clearer vision), looked through the superimposition and testified to seeing the finished Kingdom *here, at hand.* The discerning Jesus continually called attention to the perfect world as *now* in our midst.

Individual consciousness interprets the perfect Creation in degrees, "line upon line, precept upon precept, here a little, and there a little," and as vision enlarges, one beholds more and more completely the perfection which is prepared.

Take, for instance, the material ways of locomotion. Instead of being instantly where one wishes to be, (as Jesus perfectly demonstrated), there came to this world at one time the vision of the stage-coach. Then as clearer spiritual vision followed this was interpreted, or represented variously and successively by the steam engine, the electric engine, the automobile and the aeroplane.

Today the aeroplane is man's exhibit of his highest concept of instantaneity. With a little more clearing of the mist there will come even a fleeter and more easily constructed device, and later man will find something no larger than his own body which will carry him easily and swiftly over land and water. Finally the greater Light will reveal that one can carry his own body triumphantly through space, directed only by his own thought and will.

Today rapid progress is seen in all manner of inventions, discoveries, facilities of all kinds and natures, and this progress in material ways is taking place only because of the *great advance in spiritual vision*. Multitudes all over the world are applying their vision of Reality, of the perfect Creation, of the Jesus Christ presence to the transcendence of all false beliefs, and day by day we are reaching that Vision which sees *face to face*.

This spiritual Vision of oneself as free, flawless being blesses the mental plane and mind begins to take on new thought and new ideas. Brotherhood is expressed as never before; a blending of hearts is being observed, not only with individuals but with countries and with nations.

Spiritual vision blesses, too, the physical plane of action. Both mental and physical planes are controlled by spiritual understanding. People are eating, dressing differently, appearing differently everywhere; everything, everyone, constantly rising from glory to glory.

Said the prophet Isaiah:

"Woe unto them that call evil good, and good evil; that put darkness for light and light for darkness."

Since the world, as far as we are concerned, is our consciousness of it, evil and good are terms which mean to one his concept of them. One who knows in his heart the allness of good (because of the allness of God) undertakes not to expound to a brother, unenlightened by Truth, the nothingness of evil, but he preaches to him *Repentance.*

Repent of what? Those who believe that erring sense is reality and power must repent and forsake this false view, for not until one spiritually perceives the allness and everpresence of good does he claim and comprehend the nothingness, (in itself), of evil.

To call evil good and good evil is to be double-visioned,—is to see both good and evil as power. As one worships and understands Reality, he discards untrue belief and refuses temptation. Spiritual healing is Spirit conscious of Its totality. Any superimposition, any erring condition that one seems to manifest can be dissipated by the living Truth, by Christ consciousness. Spiritual healing is evidence that all discord and limitation are unreal.

Jesus cast out false beliefs because of the Truth *in himself*. When it is stated that the world exists in us, that our world is our consciousness of it, it means that whatever *we* accept as reality, as power, as presence, constitutes *our* world at that time.

The following is an example. A woman, on a

busy street in the city, suddenly noticed a great crowd of people collected, blocking traffic. Moving along until she saw the cause of the commotion, her eyes reported an accident. A horse and automobile had come together and a man lay underneath.

Now as this woman looked, this panorama of excitement, commotion and accident, was reported to her external world,—her eyes; but she heard a Voice very close at hand, the voice of her inner world and it said: "Never mind what these people are seeing, what are you seeing?"

"Yes, what am I seeing?" she quickly asked herself. "Why,—why, I am seeing heaven," she cried joyously, unconsciously moving away. "There are no accidents in *my* world. In *my* world there is eternal changeless order and delight." The incident was wiped absolutely from her mind as happily she continued her way.

Several weeks later, she happened to meet a friend who, not knowing she had been near the scene of the disaster, began relating it to her, stating that she had stood in the crowd and had seen "the whole thing." "And the strangest thing of all happened," she went on. "Suddenly it all seemed to be over. The people seemed to be on their way without any departure; the horse became quiet; the trampled man stood up refusing assistance; and the havoc and excitement changed to order and normality like a miracle." But that other, the one who walked in her own world, she knew and understood for in her world she had seen *face to face*.

It is inherent in each individual to know himself, to express himself, to *be* himself. As individual perception coalesces with true Consciousness, false belief slips from mind as a dream, and manifestation is seen in its true light. Thus, one sees creation according to his individual state of consciousness. One sees the so-called outer world according to his spiritual awakening.

In which world are *we* living? Are we living

in a material world affected by every wind that blows, believing what eyes report, what ears hear and what mind sanctions?

Or, are we living in a perfect world, visioning with eyes of Spirit, listening with ears attuned to Truth, functioning with mind which is none other than the mind of Christ?

Truly our world is our consciousness of it. It is not a question with us, how much wrong thinking, wrong living there is in it, rather is it a question with each of us, How much true belief have we accepted into our consciousness?

It has been truly said: "Without vision the people perish." Without vision of the spiritual perfect universe, the Kingdom within the Soul, the people perish. For, visioning outward things, such as purport to be sickness, sin, death, is it any wonder that one should perish by reason of these very things which he visions?

Let us bring our light into our world and let it shine. Let us see no separation, destruction or opposition, but only Oneness, Unity, Omnipresence. So shall resurrection take place in you and in me, and as resurrection takes place in us this glory from on high shall illumine our whole universe and all of our affairs.

We come not forth to battle with darkness, either with thoughts or weapons. Light eliminates darkness laborlessly. We do not make a wall between light and darkness but bring false beliefs right into the presence of our true Self. *"I am the Light"* cried the invincible Jesus. This Light is within you, within me,—the Light that will lighten any darkened sense, for Self is light and to be Self is to be light.

Jesus continually turned his vision to the Light, his true perfect Being. This enabled him to transcend and transmute experiences of this world, and led him to resurrection and ascension

Jesus, in the apparent giving up of his sense of life, demonstrated *eternality of Consciousness.* God could not die, neither could Jesus. He could die to appearance, die to a double-visioned universe, but he could not die *to himself.*

Verily, this was the claim of Jesus: *"I am the atonement! I am the resurrection! I am the ascension!*

We have entered a period of a tremendous awakening. Progress and revelation such as the world has never before known has appeared to human consciousness. This is the day of the emancipation of humanity. As centuries ago the Southern slave found his slavery taken from him, so are human beings today having human limitations taken from them, — limitations of time, age, disease, and discord.

These falsities of bondage and limitation are being outlawed through perception of one's spiritual, eternal, irresistible Nature.

Great inspiration and illumination are coming rapidly over the whole world. This is the age of surprises, of visions, of unexpected discoveries. Day by day, hour by hour, heaven comes closer to the race consciousness. The signs of the times can now be read quite easily by one of insight. Music, for instance, is rapidly assuming wider and wider proportions until soon music will be recognized as fourth dimensional. No longer do we find music confined to four walls, but now we hear it in the streets, in the market places, in the automobiles and even up over our heads in the sky. We can scarcely find a place where the burst of a song or a melody does not come upon our ears.

Often too it is reported that one hears tones other than those from the radio; he hears the music from the super-world. Such melody is un-dimensional, unlimited, unconfined. It is to be expected that in this Era of Insight, or Era of spiritual Light, many wonderful things unheard of heretofore shall come to pass. Great changes are noticed taking place in governments, racial beliefs, creeds and rituals.

As we contact the true idea of a thing the

false idea drops away *automatically*. As we lift our vision to the Self-existent Heights we surely find the reality of health, joy and glory irresistibly entering our lives and radiating through all our experience.

There is no limitation, no spot or blemish upon the face of the whole Creation. The limitation imposed by one's false belief is illusion only. Jesus reported no evil. He said that nothing shall by any means hurt us; he promised that one could handle serpents quite harmlessly; that, should one swallow poison, he need not be at all affected by the world's belief of such a procedure.

Let us acknowledge Jesus' promises to be true TODAY. Let us declare: I do believe in the word of the living Christ. I worship the One. I identify myself with Him who said that we all may be one, that the works that he did we shall do also. I have almighty and implicit faith in the spirit of Truth, in the unity of Being, in the glory of Soul.

There is one Substance in this world which is fixed, permanent, sounding down through the ages. *My words* shall not pass away. Heaven and earth shall pass away but *My Word* shall never lose its power, never fail to fulfill.

To perceive *unity*, we function from a place above reason, above the relative mentality.

Truth is above comparison! Truth is incomparable. It is not how much greater Truth is than something else, or how much greater one belief is than another belief. We do away with comparisons. We see that truth IS. When we measure our vision by this standard we find that our Kingdom is here "on earth as it is in heaven."

Let us tell ourself continually that the universe is within us, that we see without according to what we are perceiving within. We see in the mirror what is standing before the mirror. How can we expect to vision the One without, if we are not entertaining the one *within?* How can we perceive unity in the universe if we have not unity *in our consciousness?*

Yea, is it not the Christ *in you* who is your hope of glory? How should we hope to see the Christ without, if we have not yet found the Christ *within?* How many of us have failed to recognize Christ at our door, because we were not feeling Christ in our hearts?

Is not clear Insight Lord of the dark as well as of the day? Was not Jesus, Lord of earth as well as Lord of Heaven,—"*Lord of heaven and earth.*"? Lift the veil from your eyes and behold the *oneness* of life, *the unity* of being, and see no separation, division or comparison.

Truth is totality! Truth is therefore the only substance that is ever present.

One need put forth no vision to see light where light is present, but who is seeing the light which shineth in darkness?

It is easy enough to behold the Christ in the smiling countenance, the radiant Soul, but who is visioning the Christ in the darkened and unillumined mentality? It is simple to see health where health is visibly present, but who is seeing health where health is not visibly present?

It would have been easy for great multitudes to have accepted Jesus as the Christ had he been born in a palace, but how few accepted him who was born in a manger!

It is easy for one to be brave and strong in the midst of harmony and peace, but how many of us are brave and strong in the midst of mighty trials, temptations and dangers?

Who comes forth from the fiery flames with no smell of smoke upon his clothing? Who feels the everlasting arms underneath while falling into an abyss of darkness? Who hears the angel's voice in the midst of his soul's darkest moment? Who sees dry land in the midst of the Red Sea?

He who has vision! He who has faith! He who has trust! He who has love! He who is visioning face to face.

CHAPTER IV.

PRACTICAL DEMONSTRATION

MEN, great as poets, mystics, saints and reformers, are men of renunciation. They have renounced personality. They are not swayed by opinions nor moved by praise or censure. They look to the Light shining in their own souls.

The bird does not trust to the twig that sways beneath his light weight upon it. He trusts to his wings. We may have houses and lands, friends and families, but we place not our trust in these; we place not our happiness and our safety here. We remember: "All my trust on Thee (Understanding) is stayed."

Truth is the health of our body; Truth is the breath of our Life; Truth is the sparkle of our eyes, the laughter of our lips, the strength of our hands. How close Truth is to us. Hark! Listen to the robin. It is the One singing his song. The One is the beauty of the flower, the charm of the evening, the breath of the morning, the pulse of all being. Yea, the One is All in all.

No matter how far one may have wandered in the dream, no matter how low one may have fallen in belief, a welcome is ready for him who cries, "*I will arise and go to my Father.*" The wayward son in the parable left his home of joy and abundance and started off to search life for himself. Time and experience brought him nothing but husks, unrest, disappointment. Finally he remembered how happy he had been with his father; what a comfortable home he had had there; how care-free and joyous he had been. Ah, what a fool to have left! What ignorance to have chosen darkness rather than light; husks rather than real Substance. *He would return.*

But wait, how would he be received? Notwithstanding this doubt he would go at once. And he returned just as he was, poor, weak, weary, heartsick, miserable in both mind and body.

And lo, he found everything the same as before he left. The moving the hands of the clock had not changed a thing. All was the same as if he had never wandered away at all. Now he accepts the genuine substance; he lives the life his father desires; and he finds peace, joy and glory. He has now "put on" that which was ALREADY for his acceptance!.

It is like this with us. We oftimes forget our first awakening, our first blaze of glory and our spontaneous gladness which, like a sparkling spring, bubbles from the living well within. Let us not abandon that vision of oneness enabling us to walk over waves and through Red seas.

Is it not in recognizing the finished Kingdom at hand, in accepting the Christ within, in speaking the Truth in His Name, and in practicing the presence of the One, that we grow more and more familiar with the Science of Ascension?

Remember it is the heart and not the head that makes such things possible. The question for us all to consider and answer is, *Am I practicing the Presence of the One?*

Does not the One ask, "Can you hear My voice if you are looking to personality for guidance and uplift?" Books and teachers of Truth deliver a light which enables one in a wonderful way to see this Truth in his own heart. They help one to place his radical reliance upon Christ as the almighty Power, the changeless and imperishable Reality.

We bring the sense of a separate, or personal state, to the Impersonal, or God-state, and we begin a new Life. Laying down the untrue for the true, the limited for the actual, the temporal for the eternal, we find the peace of God which passeth (human) understanding.

We hear the Voice: "I came to earth as Jesus

Christ to show you how to transcend the human state, the earth-state, and how to perceive and accept your perfect God-being."

"But why is this dream-state necessary?" you ask. "Why am I seeing that which is called time, space, personality, sin, sickness and discord?"

"If Intelligence did not manifest as such, what were the use then of Intelligence? If Power were inert, dormant, unexpressed, of what avail then were that Power? If Love were unknown, unfelt, untold, of what delight were such Love? Can you not recall that when you have been lifted on high, when you have received great illumination, when sickness has rolled back like dew before the sun, when sorrow has subsided like darkness before the light, that THIS has been the moment when you were transfused with raptuous joy, with unutterable peace, power and glory? Then you have *known* Truth. Then you have *felt* Love. Then you have *manifested* even that which you are,—Myself."

Now it may seem to the unenlightened consciousness that one is a human being born of human parents and that through experience one progresses to health, joy and peace. However, the announcement of Truth, the Gospel of Jesus, proclaims that inherently we are divine beings *now*; that the road called progress and experience does not *create* our perfection but rather does it DISCLOSE and REVEAL our perfection.

Today on every hand we find people searching for health. This is similar to one searching for the glasses which rest upon his nose; like one dying of hunger while gold fills his purse. Searching, traveling and seeking *externally* takes one in a wrong direction. He seeks that which he already is. The River of the water of Life abides in him and is his everlasting health.

Jesus left a message, Behold, the Kingdom of everlasting life is here, at hand. Look thou upon the fields *already* white to harvest!

Therefore we find that the true Way, or the

illumined Path, is not something to be attained externally, but rather is it something to be inwardly revealed. Christ stands in our midst saying, "Peace, Be Still!" His Message is: *In you is the Water of Life. In you is the heavenly Kingdom.*

"Cast your care upon Me," says the inner Voice. The radiance and quickening inspiration is of the Holy Ghost, instantly forgiving sins or mistakes, and instantly placing the body under heavenly law. Miracles attend the coming of our Christ. Never doubt but that *your* hour of fulfillment is at hand. Lifting our vision to spiritual Reality, we find this Reality entering our being and all of our affairs. Our minds, renewed and refreshed, are filled with joyous praise and glory. We find it a very easy thing now to be absent from the body and present with our Lord-self.

A falsity, of course, has no substance back of it,—nothing to hold or sustain it and its fabulous existence is bound to be discovered. The redemption of mental darkness consists in accepting the light of Truth.

There is told a story of some savages who lived in a dark cave in a certain part of the Himalayas. They had never seen the light of a fire. These savages cooked their food as best they could by the heat of the sun; they went to bed and arose the day following by solar light. As time went on, they began to wish that they might see what was in the depths of this great cave in which they lived. Day by day they longed to drive out this terrible darkness, and they believed that evil spirits and great monsters were moving around here; in fact, they imagined that they saw them.

Some one told them that this terrible monster —Darkness—would leave if they would worship it. They followed this suggestion faithfully; they beseeched and supplicated the darkness, but it remained as unyielding as before. Then they were told to fight this dark being,—to take clubs and strike and beat it into submission. However, with their clubs and weapons they did but strike one another, and this device was soon abandoned as unfeasible. They also tried fasting and other practices but all to no end. The darkness was as great as ever.

Finally a man came along who told them that the only thing that could make darkness leave was a light. This man asked for some straw and bamboo sticks, and by striking a stone against a piece of flint there came a spark. Soon by means of the twigs and straws the long bamboo stick began to blaze. The savages now followed this man as he entered the great black cave and lo, *the darkness was not there!*

They thoroughly searched the cave but could find no evil spirits, no monsters, nor could they find the darkness for wherever they carried the light, behold, there was only light. At last their wish was granted. The darkness left.

Now after one has perceived the true Light and after this Light has taken away some of his darkness, he can never again believe so completely in that darkness as reality. It is this way after one has glimpsed the finished Kingdom. Never again is a world of time, space and personality quite so real to him. As one passes above the plane of thought and looks up and out into the perfect Land, he *automatically* becomes filled with new ecstacy and new joy that never before has been equalled in his experience.

This land of prepared glory which he now beholds is one in which there is no separation of people, things or ideas whatsoever. Here one is unbounded, unlimited, free as air. Here beautiful thoughts come bubbling from one like sparkling elixir. One sees a universe of truth and love; of joyous splendor and ever-increasing glory. No suggestion of sin, of fear, of sickness or destruction is thought here, for this is the realm of perfect light; this is the realm of ideal harmony; this is the heavenly Kingdom; this is the place of the heart.

Now after one has experienced such inspiration —the lighting of the fire within the self, the removal of the darkness—he finds that spiritual affirmations become more and more alive to him. No longer do sentences mean mere words to him, —like so many letters of the alphabet joined together,—but now they take on fresh meaning. Something even seems shining upon the pages of the book which he is reading and the words are like living things. One feels a great expansion, a freedom and an independence not known before.

After one has caught glimpses of the finished Kingdom, a new language is his, a new tongue. Many words now reveal new meaning to him; for instance, the word *health*. One used to think of health as identified with the body, but now he sees that Health is universal and is on the mountain top or in the dungeon. Health is unlimited and omnipresent like the sunshine, and like the fact that two and two are four. Health is a fact of Being. Health is indivisible Omnipresence.

The word *health* is placed with great words such as *infinity, eternity, freedom, life, love, peace and power.* We vision a perfect universe; we behold a living Christ; we believe that good and abundance, health and harmony are of a universal Substance.

Not by strength of body nor by might of mind but *by My Spirit*, saith our Lord-Self. Now the spirit of the Lord in one is perfect ideal being. The spirit of the Lord is that health which is in everything but attached to nothing, for Health is Reality.

Spirit is the fact that "The desert shall rejoice, and blossom as the rose . . . the eyes of the blind shall be opened, and the ears of the deaf shall be unstopped . . . the lame man shall leap . . . and the tongue of the dumb shall sing." Spirit is the fact that there is no limit of health to the body, no limit of understanding to the mind. There is no division, no limitation, no attachment in being.

Spirit is the fact that there is no stopping place

for life, no boundary to health, no termination for joy, peace or delight. Spirit is the fact that we are living NOW and that this life will never cease for one instant to *be*; that we are a being of Intelligence, Power, Glory, without end; that we are divine, eternal, irresistible Soul, Self, Truth.

We drink the Water of Life freely, and the path of Illumination shines bright with living glory. The presence of the One is seen, known, felt and understood. The Golden Age is here— the Age of boundless Freedom, of indescribable Splendor, Love and Glory.

God-being is not subject to material law any more than a bird is subject to the laws governing vegetables. We recognize, affirm and declare, that we as God-being are not subject to the laws of matter, but that we *are free in heavenly Reality*. With burning zeal and with fire of insight we insist that we are immune from all sense of evil, bondage and limitation. Jesus declared that none of these things, (material beliefs), could harm us for there is no harm in unreality.

The conditions pictured in the body, and called dis-ease, are not at all as they seem to unenlightened vision. The report of the senses is that the dis-ease is in or on the body, that the trouble is *external*. This is altogether an erroneous idea, for what is seen in the body and termed disease is *picture* only, and is no more in the body than a horse pictured on the motion picture screen is on the screen. The perception of this one point, alone, brings great relief and freedom.

As we correct untrue thoughts, (darkness), with right, spiritual ideas, (light), simultaneously the picturization changes and instead of disease, (darkness), there is now health, (light).

Let us acquaint ourself with true spiritual ideas. One of the first to establish as a working basis is that *we are Spirit, God.* This fact accepted, it is then easy to perceive that *spiritual* being is not subject to false beliefs. A God-being cannot believe falsely, but is forever conscious of harmony and changeless reality.

No false picture exists in the mind of Christ and our heritage is this Mind. What harm can a false thing do? We perceive that Truth is with us and so nothing can be against us. We realize that a false idea is no idea at all; we cease fearing it.

Filling our consciousness with divine ideas— ideas of reality, of love, of peace, of omnipotence, of victory—we ask, "What is there that can hinder us from expressing that marvelous being which we *are*? What is there to keep us from that wonderful glory which is *ready* and *prepared* for us? Can anything oppose Almighty Truth? Can anything prevent our response when Almighty Truth claims us?

We insist that, being Soul, we cannot lose our vision of eternal, changeless and harmonious existence. Our vision is clear and constant. Our ideas are pure and complete. Our bodies are one with true consciousness, hence they are free from all falsity and from all imperfection whatsoever.

Pictures can move rapidly on the picture screen yet nothing is actually taking place on the *screen*; nothing is being healed, or removed, or changed. Attention is given to the *machine* (mind) and the picture (expression) follows automatically.

Perceiving that there is no kingdom of darkness, that the kingdom within us is the Kingdom of *everlasting Light*, we arise new-born. We shout our freedom from limitation; we hold fast to reality, and we say, "What can separate us from the all-Power? What can overthrow the omnipotence of our divinity?

Thus, correcting material beliefs with spiritual ideas, we commence to experience a new world. We have not created our health and harmony but *we have taken possession of them*. We have awakened to the fact of the perfect health and harmony *at hand*.

Surely there is a power irresistible, able to do all things. Let those of us who are seeing and feeling this light bring it to other hearts longing and waiting for its arrival. The presence of the living Truth is sweeping this universe, making itself known, seen, felt, hour by hour, ushering in the Golden Age wherein are boundless freedom, indescribable splendor, irresistible love and transcendent glory.

You are not divided into a soul, a mind and a body. The body is the means through which Soul, being, brings itself into expression, action. Body is as imperishable, undefilable, indestructible, everlasting, eternal as Being, for *Being and body are one.* We are Being, action, form. We cannot be separated, divided, disunited. Creator, creating and creation comprise one unit.

Let all sense of division and separateness depart from thought. We are not trying to unite God and man, Soul and body, for clear vision reports that God and man, Soul and body, Cause and effect, Life and form, *are one now, always, and forever.*

Every hour earth is taking on more of the glory of Heaven, and from glory to glory we press forward. Deserts are becoming fertile, valleys are blossoming forth. Cities, countries, nations are daily uniting in thought and the result will be peace and power. We are facing the seventh angel, the day of fulfillment and rest.

Let us acknowledge that the time is come, the hour is here. The Angel of Insight gently whispers *"Be of good cheer"* over all the earth. The Bible instructs us that the body is transformed by the renewing baptism of Spirit; therefore, being-new-born in Spirit and putting on (accepting) our inherent immortality we gently and laborlessly transcend inharmonious experience. Mind imbued with spiritual understanding is a law unto itself, dispelling illusions and blotting out erring beliefs.

When Spirit is seen and accepted to be the

life of all, when it is certain to us that we all have the same life, the same being, the same reality, then the divine body will appear.

Progress is a term applied to human existence wherein the sense called mortal, through states and stages of consciousness, progresses to the point of ascension—the final triumph over all beliefs of mortal being and mortal universe.

Spirit is not regenerated. It is humanity that is regenerated. How can we understand God except through spiritualization of thought? Dematerialization and spiritualization is one process. In this process of vision, and practical demonstration, sense (mortality) seems to pass through three distinct stages before yielding completely to Truth (immortality). These three stages are called the *atonement*, the *resurrection* and the *ascension*.

Atonement is the dawning upon human consciousness of one's sinless, perfect state. Atonement is perception that as "Light shineth *in* darkness," it is therefore impossible for evil to be evil. One perceives that inasmuch as the universe is primarily in one's consciousness, there is therefore no *external* evil. What is called evil is like the cloud that would conceal the light. The light shines, constantly and uninterruptedly.

Always the good is shining in consciousness but when mists of sense obscure the good then the result has been termed "evil." Atonement, therefore, is perception of *one* Presence as *always* present. It is perception that all that changes is *belief*. That which has been called evil, (such as disease, destruction and death), are the results of false sense—results of not clearly perceiving the light which is always shining.

Atonement perceives that correction is to take place inwardly. The "outward" follows automatically. That which needs correction is mistaken sense. One perceives that untrue (false) beliefs are to be corrected by the acceptance in our consciousness of genuinely true ideas.

Resurrection, the second step leading from sense to Soul, is the *practice* of atonement, Resurrection is *practical demonstration*. Resurrection is restoration,—the restoring to the mind of power, might, glory and dominion; the restoring of that which was never lost or lacking except in belief. Resurrection is the *practice* of right vision and the *practice* of right ideas.

Resurrection is self-improvement in sense and thought. As higher and higher concepts of health and immortality are delivered, naturally one embodies and expresses them. It is this living process of resurrection that has been called *"practicing the Presence."*

Resurrection is the period delivering abatement of so-called evil. It is self-purification; it is awakening from the dream of "opposites" to the perception and acceptance of oneness.

Ascension is one's utter renunciation of all that constitutes mortality, and it is the attainment in consciousness of one's eternal individual identity.

Ascension is the return in belief, of the Prodigal to his Father's home—his real state of Being. Having taken the footsteps of atonement (right perception of reality and unreality), and having taken the step following called resurrection (practice of the One as All), the Prodigal (mortal) has entirely lost his sense of mortality and has gained the sense of spiritual pre-existence. He now enters his spiritual rest and finds eternal peace.

As we learn the way in Absolute Science and enlarge our Spiritual capacity for a higher life, we individualize sovereign power and demonstrate the falsity of bondage and limitation.

The Science of Ascension, revealed to the waiting heart, opens prison doors to those who are bound and sets the captive free.

Spiritual ideas delivering to us a spiritual sense, lead us to divine Heights and make it possible for us to exchange a material sense of existence for Soul-existence. As consciousness is uplifted, one gently relinquishes untrue beliefs and notions, demonstrating his divine authority in overcoming sin, sickness and discord.

Exercising his inherent Authority one rises to the enraptured perception of Self as dwelling in infinite harmony,—complete, perfect, immutable and incorruptible.

As material sense,—the sense reporting pain, limitation, discord, is perceived as *false,* and as Spiritual sense—the sense of health, joy and harmony is recognized the *real* sense, one begins to utilize his infinite power to establish in his daily experience a perfectly harmonious existence.

We are delivered to Truth as we accept and embody Truth. This is not a method of mind over matter, nor is it mind over mind, but it is the divine process of *spiritualizing thought and sense,* demonstrating the omnipotence of Truth over false beliefs and enforcing the spiritual act of Soul over false sense. Truth is victorious, supreme and gloriously omnipotent. The consciousness of this fact redeems sense from fear, renews faith and exalts the affections.

Gaining the vision of self as eternal Life, irresistible Truth, and exalting Love, we lose fear and boldly enforce our Understanding.

Beholding the truth of our being and accepting our heritage—our reality as the Christ-Self—we unhesitatingly stand firm in our faith, knowing that the Holy Ghost dwells with us.

What is the ultimate of so-called attainment but *ascension?* Is this not the victory that is prepared for us,—the overcoming of all belief in sin, sickness, limitation, and the crowning triumph over death? Not a thing but false sense conceals Reality from us and not a thing but spiritualization of thought and vision opens to us the gates of Paradise, revealing ascension above earthly sense.

What can melt away the sense of fear and darkness except the understanding of true being? Understanding is the Light which places the feet on firm ground, establishing its Principle by demonstration.

The Kingdom of all-inclusive good never disappeared from Spiritual sight but remains forever intact, omnipresent and tangible to immortal Consciousness.

The Kingdom of eternal uninterrupted harmony awaits individual recognition and acceptance. In proportion as human consciousness becomes divine is the perfection and completeness of Self realized and embodied. Clad with divine illumination and spiritual perception, we assert our mastery over disease, fear and bondage and we prove irrefutably that divine Understanding is supreme and triumphant. Waking to the perception of self as God-being, we are lifted to a higher plane of experience and find it possible to demonstrate health and harmony.

The awakened consciousness sees but one way—the Self. *"I am the Way."* Truth leads the eager and ready heart onward and upward, advancing it spiritually, and disclosing the ultimate perception that the Kingdom of everlasting harmony and glory is *within one's own power and demonstration.*

Practical demonstration is the act of Truth destroying material beliefs and uplifting faith and vision to discern perfect Creation, *permanent, changeless,* untouched by any dream sense. As Reality is brought to light, human sense is resurrected and the spiritual idea of life is revealed as ever-operative and practical.

Those instructed in Absolute Science have grasped the glorious view of Self as all-knowing, all-mighty, and all-inclusive; and practicing this inspiring view they ascend the scale of being and emerge gently into Life everlasting.

Let us know and demonstrate that an improved belief cannot retrograde. Once we gain control of erring sense through Soul or spiritual understanding let us stand firm and unfaltering, realizing that nothing can deprive us of our complete demonstration of health, harmony and happiness.

All there is to sickness, sin and death is a false claim, a claim of falsity which cannot dethrone Soul, or deprive any one of his continuous sense of life and immortality. There is but one right Vision—the fact of perfect Being, perfect ideas, and perfect expression. Holding thought to this Ideal we master so-called material law and annul its erring sentence. This divine practice, in its direct application to human needs, lifts individual consciousness above physical sense, removes fear and false belief, and reveals the all-power and ever-presence of our Kingship and Kingdom.

Absolute Science, lifting one's consciousness higher in the scale of being, reveals to him that identifying himself as Christ he is free, victorious and triumphant.

This spiritual understanding discloses individual might and power and reveals the phenomenon of Ascension.

CHAPTER V.

Right Interpretation

IT is stated that one can easily penetrate and expose un-truth when he perceives the genuine and real; when he perceives the truth itself.

As soon as an un-truth comes to one's attention, intuitively he feels the impulse to investigate the *truth* of the situation, for he knows that if he can discover the truth, the un-truth will automatically be exposed and annulled.

Should some one bring information that does not seem true to us and we wish to ascertain if his report is actually true, we begin to trace his statement back to its origin or starting place, do we not? We unravel the story, little by little, until we are satisfied that we have arrived at the truth.

Looking through a veil, truth appears inverted, impossible, but stripping off the veil, we penetrate the mist and perceive the real to be real, and the unreal to be nothing.

Now it is easily understood that when a true statement is voiced or a true experience is placed before us, we do not investigate this, for there is no need of investigating harmony, peace and contentment. But when something disturbing or disconcerting comes to our attention, the first impulse is to look up the truth and find out the actual facts.

We do not attend to the report itself, nor do we attend to the false situation or condition, but exercising spiritual vision, we look *beyond* the so-called material and erring testimony, and perceive the truth that is standing back of it, the truth which seems concealed from view.

> "The light shineth in 'darkness and the darkness comprehendeth it not."—*St. John.*

If we perceive the light that is shining, we simultaneously expose the darkness which is comprehending it not. Looking toward this light and meditating, it comes to us that a condition of sleep and lapse from the actual state of being, or a condition of false and untrue belief does not accord with the words of Jesus, "*Ye* are the light. . . . The Kingdom is within *you.*" We also recognize that back of the put-to-sleep belief *there is a genuine fact of perfect, changeless being,* and back of the untrue expression of inharmony and discord *there shines the fact of perfect, changeless and immortal embodiment.*

We let not a sense of sympathy go toward the individual who claims to be experiencing falsely nor to the condition which he states is substantiating his mental claim. What is the onlooker seeing? Is he seeing the true universe truly? If so, there is no occasion for sympathy, fear or disturbance. Is he beholding form corresponding to the spiritual Vision of changeless, perfect and immaculate being? If so, he is mindful of reality.

The IDENTITY which the onlooker reports first as a crawling caterpillar and later as a beautiful butterfly never changes, for individual identity is Self and is therefore constant, un-changeable and immortal, no matter what any onlooker may be claiming.

This fact perceived, one grasps it so exultantly that he begins at once to interpret the universe according to reality.

Recognizing and accepting individual identity as forever established, perfect and complete, without beginning and without end, he now perceives that any untrue expression presenting itself to physical vision and testifying to discord, disease and disturbance is at variance with the premise and the principle of this changeless identity, and therefore cannot be accepted as carrying a vestige of truth.

No matter what may be the testimony of

material sense, no matter what may be the testimony of darkness comprehending not the light, the fact is *that perfect being and perfect universe are now at hand for us to behold and experience.*

Let it be clearly perceived that a being who at one time is called a *mortal* and at another time is called an *immortal is one entity. A mortal is not an immortal* but this relative statement is understood as one correctly interprets it. It can be said that a caterpillar is not a butterfly, yet the onlooker knows that though *he* calls one form by a certain term, and at another time by another term, *he is all the time referring to the same entity.*

Thus with individual being. With a clouded view, being is interpreted as mortal and human, while with spiritual vision, being is interpreted as perfect and divine. *The individual identity, however, is uninterrupted, constant and eternal.*

When one is believing in something that is untrue, believing some false condition present which actually is not here, this state of mind is called in metaphysics "false belief." It is this false belief that one has to meet and overcome—and he meets and overcomes it with the right, with the Truth, with right interpretation.

Relatively speaking, that which causes darkness to disappear from a room is the light, and relatively, that which causes false or untrue belief to disappear from the mind is true belief. Belief in Truth is true belief and right interpretation, and as one exercises this right interpretation he finds the kingdom of heaven within his own consciousness.

A true belief has actual substance back of it. If one traces back the true belief, he arrives at the absolute Truth itself. And if one traces back the un-true belief, he sees that as untruth, it has no support whatsoever; it rests upon nothing, for it is but an untrue interpretation *of that which is perfect and true.*

This is why one need not sympathize with another who is apparently shadowing forth an un-true state. Instead of sympathizing with a mistake, a misrepresentation, one brings the light of truth to that consciousness. One understands that in accepting true belief, he has Christ with him, he has Reality with him, and his victory is assured.

Therefore, one does not treat dis-ease, sorrow or any dis-order as though it were actual, but he sees that this is the picturing forth of wrong belief in the mind, and that as soon as true belief is accepted, this Truth is the light which spontaneously illumines his universe.

Holding to the perception that we are Life, we are Truth, we are Spirit, one feels firm ground under his feet, feels omnipotent Reality within him. With eyes clear and with feet firmly planted on that which is, the un-true expression vanishes and utterly disappears.

One is not misled, however, into thinking that

any actual change has taken place for such belief is not clear perception. It is simply that now one has a fuller consciousness of reality, and he is expressing this improved belief.

"Nothing shall by any means hurt you," testified Jesus. It is as we perceive this tremendous fact of Reality and practice it in our vision, thinking and acting, that we ascend above untrue states and beliefs.

The vision of Ascension sees clearly that nothing external is to be healed, changed or removed. We do not go out with vision, thought or action to conquer dis-cord. We go *within* always. And within we find Truth. And finding Truth, we rest in the consciousness that our being is Omniscience, Omnipotence and Omnipresence. This right interpretation uplifts human understanding, and Christ appears.

The putting on of immortality is not like the putting of a cloak upon one's shoulders nor like the placing of gold into one's purse, but putting on immortality is like the receiving of something that one did not know that he already possesses. Children, for instance, "put on" *two and two are four.* It appears as though they receive it outwardly, or that they add it to their knowledge, whereas the fact is that the consciousness of this fact already exists in them.

It is written in a well-known metaphysical text book: "*Mortals will some day assert their freedom in the name of Almighty God!*" Mortals (those unillumined as to their actual perfection) are destined (because of their nature) to trace back their identity and to discover that this identity is the actual Truth.

Isaiah, looking into Reality, perceived that Jesus was the "Mighty God, the Everlasting Father," and Jesus, visioning the Kingdom of perfect Being, exclaimed, "That we all may be one."

In the story of the sheep and the lion cub, the latter lived for years as a sheep, not realizing his lion nature until a real lion presented itself before his vision; likewise, people for many centuries considered themselves mortal and human until *Reality* came before their vision and they recognized *themselves* as Reality.

In the story, the sheep-lion did not experience his real nature until he saw the majestic lion standing upon the hill-side, outlined against the horizon. Gazing enraptured at this ideal, all of a sudden he felt something give way within him, —his sheep belief vanished. Recognizing *himself* as lion, spontaneously he accepted his real nature and entered into his kingdom of the jungle and forest.

What a great lesson lies concealed in this simple parable. Covering the face of this earth were people who, believing they were human beings, experienced sickness, sin and death in accordance with their false beliefs. But one day, looking up, lo! there, standing before them, was the glorious Presence,—*"the lion of the tribe of*

Judah,"—a being of transcending glory and majesty.

Gazing rapturously at this Ideal, many felt something give way within them, their human beliefs vanished. Recognizing their God-being, spontaneously they accepted their real nature and they entered their rightful heritage,—the Kingdom of perfection.

This Ideal Presence is here TODAY, standing before all, for to those who look for him doth he appear before them! *"Lo, I am with you alway . . . I will never leave thee nor forsake thee!"*

Beloved, we *are* looking upon this Christ,—our Ideal Self! We too *have felt* that false something give way in us, delivering us from the belief that we are human beings! We *rapturously* and *spontaneously* accept our Kingship and our Kingdom!

We see deliverance before us. We behold our Kingdom at hand. We accept our Ideal standing on the Mountain peak, outlined against the glowing horizon of Victory, Triumph and Ascension. Here stands our Identity,—our Christ—with face like the sun and with raiment "as no fuller on earth could white them."

All hail! Behold our Identity, Behold our God-being!

We enter the Paradise which is prepared for us in the beginning (Genesis) and which is prepared for us in the ending (Revelation); and entering, we find the peace which passeth verbal expression.

Now in applying this sublime vision to the seeming problems of every day experience, one finds that it brings him instant freedom, joy and satisfaction to apprehend and realize the right interpretation of *time, place* and *personality*.

For instance, *time*. One often feels that he is hindered by a sense of time. He feels that next week or next year more good will be disclosed to him than *now, today*. Abundance of good may seem to him to be in the future, rather than right at hand.

What is the vision of our God-self? Does this Self establish a difference between last year and today? Between today and a year from today? Verily no. To the spiritual eye there is no division, no separation whatsoever. Whatever is true is *always* true. If it is ever true that I have abundance of all good, then this fact is true *now* and for *all* time.

The notion of separation from good is altogether false and it can be proven very easily. Recently a telephone message came to me from a student asking for help. She stated that she did not know which way to turn for supply, that always her demonstration seemed depending upon some future arrangement which never came to pass and upon certain individuals who did not fulfill her expectations. Moving away from the telephone, the first thought that came to me was this.

"One day is with the Lord as a thousand years, and a thousand years as one day."—*Peter*.

It was radiantly clear to me that if the student would be helped next week or next year, she had received this help a thousand years ago. Eternity is here and at hand, "the same yesterday, today and forever," and what is called a division of *time*, such as a day, a month and a year, is merely material interpretation of changeless Reality.

In the material sense-kingdom we have *time*, but in the Kingdom *above* the material sense, we have *Eternity*. I considered this joyously, basking in the consciousness of never-beginning, never ending Eternity; and also I know that as being is *one*, the student who asked for help was also conscious of this same Reality.

Recalling that she mentioned dependence in a business way upon those at a distance from her, I saw that distance, like time, is a false sense of belief in separation and division and this false sense had no reality at all. Infinity cannot be divided or separated. It is *one* presence. Whatever is "there" is also "here," for there and here are the same position. Always (eternity), everywhere (infinity), unlimited abundance.

Then I accepted the nothingness of personality and realized that one's demonstration does not depend upon anyone but *himself. Always, everywhere, one being.*

About an hour later, the same student called me again. She said that a wonderful experience had just come to her. A Voice had spoken to her the name of a man whom she had not seen for over twenty years. I told her to go to him. Her next report was the practical demonstration. Through the help of this man, she was able to accomplish an extraordinary and gratifying sale which for over ten years she had struggled and failed to make.

Within, one finds the jewel. One is *himself* the way. Do you recall the parable of the King and the Jewel? It seems that a certain king one day came upon a stone, sparkling brilliantly in the clear waters of a lake. There before his eyes sparkled this beautiful gem. The lake was drained at the king's command, but the stone could not be found.

As soon as the water came into the lake there appeared again the sparkling of the gem. Who could fathom this mystery? A sage was called into counsel and he immediately practiced right interpretation.

Calling a servant to him, the sage commanded that he climb a tall tree growing by the side of the lake. In its overhanging branches was found a crow's nest, and here among the sticks at the bottom of the nest rested *the sparkling gem*. What was seen in the water was not the actual gem itself but only the *reflection*.

In the dream of material existence one feels that he must seek hither and yonder. He must wait for the years to roll by. He must meet certain friends or individuals who are to help him on his way toward prosperity and happiness. But he is looking in the wrong direction; he is not practicing right interpretation for he is looking out instead of *in*. The jewel is not in the outer expression. The jewel is *within*. The priceless, sparkling jewel is the Soul, is the Self. Looking within, one sees that *always, everywhere*, there is but *One being*.

Seeing and feeling this, confidently, calmly, soon the reflection appears in the universe (lake or mirror) before us. But we are not deceived. We see the sparkle, we rejoice in the demonstration, but we know that the jewel is within, we know that expression and realization are one and inseparable.

How can we experience transcending harmony and practical demonstration except by the right interpretation of Ascension? How can we exercise divine Authority except by the illumination of spiritual sense?

This exalted spiritual sense is exercised through

the inspiration of the heart. The spiritual power of glorified thought and vision, with no mental argument whatsoever, redeems one from false sense of imperfection.

There is a way above the path of trial and suffering. Reaching a higher sense through insight and revelation, one is able to demonstrate the Christ and rise *spontaneously*, easily, to the spiritual consciousness of being.

Jesus restored to human consciousness the lost sense of perfection, and he established this harmony, wholeness, joy and happiness as the reality of our individual being. This divine process of right interpretation, acknowledged and accepted by the individual, enables him to subdue the material belief in sin, sickness and limitation, and to embody the triumph of Spirit.

We can see clearly enough that there is no *actual* transition from belief to understanding, but that transition, resurrection and ascension seem essential to relative experience only.

We do not deny untrue beliefs or untrue expressions with the thought of destruction. On the contrary, we use denial with the spiritual insight and conviction that no destruction is necessary. "The law (of destruction) is not made for a righteous man." (1*Tim.* 1:9).

In our night dreams, we apparently move from one place to another place, we apparently change from one idea to another idea, but waking, we see that nothing whatever has taken place and that mental action or dream action is the same as nothing happening at all.

Preserving this perception, we understand that when we put off wrong beliefs and accept true understanding, when we put off mortality and put on immortality, this is only happening in a mental experience, for real being is eternally unchangeable.

True experience is changeless, irresistible omnipresence. In the dream-experience, deliverance and emancipation from erring beliefs and erring conditions symbolize this freedom. Perfect individual identity is here, and as we waken to the perception and acceptance of this glorious fact, we behold this being in earth as in heaven.

Full consciousness of changeless being and of supernal Life brings deliverance from the dream experience called sin, sickness and death in the same way as waking from the dream at night delivers one from dream conditions.

Our refuge is Spiritual Consciousness. Our refuge is Spiritual Ascension. Jesus' final demonstration was called the *ascension* for he rose above all illusive testimony. *Ascension is the rising into full consciousness of Self as Spirit, of Self as God.*

Spiritual ascendency is spiritual power, delivering peace, glory, harmony and reality. As thought harmoniously ascends the scale of Being, one perceives that good alone is real and true and good alone is omnipresence.

Right Interpretation enables one to lift thought

above the dream-sense, and reveals to him the spiritual body which comes with the ascension.

Metaphysics is above physics, and spiritual ascendency is above mental practice, delivering to one the power and ability to rise above dreams and illusions, and the right and might to experience the heritage of glorified being.

Right interpretation reveals what unillumined eye doth not behold. The *report* that the universe is imperfect and incomplete *is false,* for the universe is the expression of Life, Truth and Love, and is as perfect, changeless and immortal as is Intelligence, Life, Being, which sustains it.

It is relatively true that a mortal is not an immortal and it is relatively true that the universe of unillumined vision is not the Kingdom of heaven. *One identity* (Self) is ever present whether one interprets this identity as perfect and divine or imperfect and defective, likewise, *one universe* is everpresent whether one interprets this universe as heavenly and glorious, or as material and discordant.

One Life, Truth, Love and one expression, embodiment, kingdom, co-exists, ceaselessly, uninterruptedly, absolutely and finally. Casting aside erring perception and executing spiritual vision, one sees that the universe before him is none other than the Kingdom of heaven, and that the entity before him is none other than the perfect being.

The universe is the expression of Life and Spirit and is therefore a spiritual and perfect universe. Apprehending and recognizing the perfect universe this right way, one laborlessly and naturally enters it.

Prophets and Saints have left different instruction pertaining to the way in which this kingdom of perfect harmony and immortality may be attained. Some have said that the way is by mental law—*"Thou shalt not."* Others have believed that the way is disclosed through tribulations, sorrows, trials. The great Master of Understanding, however, delivered the ultimatum—*the kingdom of heaven is within you!*

The individual *himself* is the way to heavenly harmony. Through *individual* perception, recognition and acceptance of Self as God, and of universe as co-existent with Self, one enters the glory of *ascension*, experiencing the kingdom of heaven on earth.

Jesus proclaimed to "mortals" their immortality, and on earth he established the Kingdom of heaven. Truth is revealed. Perfect being and perfect universe are here, and when perfect being and perfect universe are interpreted by Absolute Science they can be rightly understood.

The *Kingdom* or perfect universe, as interpreted by Jesus, *is our consciousness of health, harmony, happiness, power, glory and authority as inherent, absolute, final, present, complete.*

Taking conscious possession of the kingdom of reality *within ourselves* through spiritual ascendency, we individualize infinite power and glory, and we express unlimited health, happiness and harmony.

Spiritual blessedness is based upon the action of Truth, and *instantaneous* healing is demonstrated as one sets aside mental argument letting his enraptured sense rest in the understanding of one Presence as *all*.

Standing upon this immortal basis, one stands on reality, oneness, infinity, and his victory is assured.

The difference between the mental argument and the way of Absolute Science is that the latter has a more spiritual basis than the former. One's practical demonstration rests upon a spiritual basis as high as his understanding of it.

Permanent perfection, irresistible harmony, perpetual loveliness, constitute all phenomena of being. Spiritual sense alone can understand and interpret the healing Christ. The more fully the Science of being is understood and interpreted by the student, the higher are his demonstrations of divine power. That Absolute Science uplifts individual consciousness to a more spiritual sense of life and love, delivering health, harmony, and happiness, thousands can attest.

Absolute Science is the mighty Deliverer, the all-sufficient Presence bringing out the highest phenomena of Reality. Proportionately as one accepts and utilizes the understanding that his real nature is the divine Trinity, he brings out in individual experience the glorious results of this understanding.

Can we demonstrate health and glorified being instantaneously, unless our own consciousness is inspired with devotion, love and revelation? Can we give living waters to the thirsty unless our own hearts are overflowing with the miracle of divine glory?

The fire of inspiration and illumination, purifying sense with Soul, forms the coincidence of the human and divine. Through divine revelation, insight and demonstration, the untrue view (materiality) disappears, and the reality or individual spiritual ideality — (Christ) — appears.

Right interpretation of the perfect universe reveals harmonious existence at hand. Looking at the ideal and interpreting it erroneously, one may call perfect Creation *matter, illusion, counterfeit*, but let it be clearly understood that the perfect Being and the Universe are co-existent and eternal. The individual view-point, the individual interpretation of this perfect Kingdom, determines for one the nature of his present individual experience.

This fact clearly and forcefully sets before all the tremendous importance that we exercise right interpretation.

Now, one may call the beautiful, glorious, heavenly universe in which we live, *matter, falsity*, and he may follow this false view with another false view,—the denial of matter, evil, falsity. But Right Interpretation delivers the insight that nothing whatever is gained by denying a thing which has no existence.

The fact is that we all live, move and act in one perfect universe, and as we spiritually perceive and accept this marvelous certainty, and individually conform our thinking and acting to this right consciousness, simultaneously our experience is harmonious, glorious and divine.

There is no necessity to deny a material universe *for there is no material universe*. The only universe there is for all, is the one established, finished, complete, perfect Kingdom.

Erroneously interpreting this finished Kingdom in which all dwell,—calling the good in this Kingdom "evil" and the divine and glorious "material," and "changeable,"—one's wrong vision prevents him from consciously experiencing the glories before him and encourages him to report a false world and a false experience.

How important then is right vision, right interpretation and right understanding! Through the Science of Ascension, we accept the facts of perfect being and perfect universe as *now* and *here* and we discard all notion of matter, evil and destruction. We perceive that it is useless and of no practical value whatsoever to deny evil, rather do we deny that there is evil. The same right perception is applied to matter, to sickness, to sin and death.

Interpreting the universe rightly, we see that there is no necessity or advantage in denying matter, sickness, sin, death, for these conditions are not found in this perfect Kingdom in which we are living. *Who convinceth spiritual Vision of sickness, sin and death?* Yea, the acknowledgment of the omnipresence and omnipotence of perfect changeless being, and perfect changeless experience, *includes* the only right denial.

The full consciousness of perfect, continuous and changeless being and of perfect, continuous and harmonious expression, *demonstrates the nothingness of sickness, sin and evil.* This spiritual action or demonstration is Ascension, for, here, the Self consciously perceives and expresses Glory, Power, Perfection and Harmony.

CHAPTER VI.

Paradise

PARADISE is within us. Our consciousness of health, joy, peace, glory, abundance, immortality is our Paradise.

Spiritualization of thought and vision is the practice of prayer, and it is this practice which delivers us to the experience of peace, joy and harmony. One is redeemed from so-called laws of the flesh as he *thinks, feels* and *acts* in the finished Kingdom. This is the way in which Soul controls sense, and the way in which Paradise is brought to light.

On the plane where progress appears to have an effect, our immunity from so-called evil is based upon our perception of reality and unreality, and upon our ability to pray, or treat, correctly.

Having established as a foundation in our consciousness the fact that our individual identity is the actual Truth, and having accepted further that all untrue belief can be corrected by spiritual understanding, we begin to ascertain how to pray, or treat, so that deliverance from erring beliefs may be quick and certain.

How can we rise in the strength of Spirit unless we ARE Spirit? How can we execute power unless we ARE Power? How can we manifest Reality unless WE ARE Reality? How can we hope to rise above discord and limitation unless we rise above the belief that the body is subject to discord and limitation? In order to laborlessly rise to our nativity in Spirit we must apprehend our actual state, (immortality), and enforce it.

How can we rise above limitation unless we are the Unlimited? How can we control erring sense unless we are Understanding? How can we remember our perfect state unless we are Intelligence? How can we hope to overcome all fear and limitation unless we perceive *that we are God-being*?

Do we not have to know that two and two are four before we can agree that two and two are not five? Must not the understanding of our *actual* being precede our understanding that we are not material beings and therefore are not subject to material, mortal beliefs? Most certainly.

One may take the figures 2 and 2 in adding, call the sum 5, but with a correct view one calls the sum 4. The figures 2 and 2 remaining the same, all that is undergoing change is the belief in the mind of the individual.

The figure 5 in the answer might stand for what is called a "mortal, or human, being" and the figure 4 might stand for an immortal, spiritual being. When untrue belief operates, the answer is untrue; and when true belief or understanding operates, the answer is true.

Now we have the problem of our own existence before us. Its beginning (Genesis) is God, and its ending (Revelation) is God. The problem that is set before us is this: *Since God is the beginning and God is the ending, what are we?*

When untrue belief operates the answer is untrue (a mortal appearance); and when true belief operates the answer is true (Immortal being).

When one believes that the answer to the mathematical problem is 5, he writes this down; and when one believes that he is a mortal (or human) being, subject to discord and limitation, he externalizes this idea. But all the time, no matter whether one is seeing rightly or wrongly, the answer is fixed, final, sure.

When one lying on his couch, dreams that he is in Europe walking on foreign pavements, what manner of being is that one who is thus portrayed in the dream? In one breath we can say,

"That man walking on the streets of Europe doesn't exist!" But with another view, we can trace that non-existent being back to the man upon the couch. Is this not so? We perceive one entity only,—*the one on the couch.*

Preserving this same viewpoint and this same procedure of vision, we begin our problem with perfect individual, spiritual being. From all about us we hear reports of pain, destruction, poverty, sorrow, disease, death. In one breath again we can declare, "But that body is a dream body and doesn't actually exist." Yet, adopting another view we say, "That may be so, but I'll trace this mind which is reporting untruly," and I'll discover its starting place. And lo! in looking back to Beginning, one comes *face to face with Reality.*

So we see, whichever way we look, whatever process of vision we adopt, we face the facts that the untrue belief and untrue expression are nothing and that the *Truth is all.*

Clear vision perceives that when the man on

the couch is conscious that he *is* on the couch, (self-conscious), he is un-conscious that he is on the streets in Europe, and simultaneously the dream picture of him as being there is gone. Also, as an individual is conscious that he is God-being, (Self-conscious), he is un-conscious that he is a material being subject to sin, disease and discord, and simultaneously the dream picture of sin, sickness and death is gone.

Becoming conscious that our life and our being is wholly Spirit, God, (for there is no other Life or Spirit), we are Self-conscious, and this divine process of spiritual perception and realization is called "spiritual healing." Thought has now ascended, and material belief has yielded to spiritual understanding.

It is said that the stream rises as high as its source. Likewise if we are to return to our Father, or perfect state, as portrayed by the parable of the prodigal, let us see what this state is. If we are to return to perfection in consciousness, it is because we already ARE perfection. If we are to return to our God-state, it is because we ARE God-being.

If one, dreaming himself upon the streets of Europe, can rise as high as his source, and his source is the man on the couch, let him see that he IS the one on the couch and his dream is gone. If one dreaming himself in a material universe, can rise as high as his source, and his source is the one Being, let him see that he IS the one Being and his dream will cease.

It seems that we are confronted with the paradox of returning to a "land" which we have never left. We are face to face with the problem of putting on the true and the "putting off" the untrue, when the fact is as Jesus so simply stated:

> "Ye ARE the Light . . . Labor NOT . . . The Kingdom is within YOU."

"Mortals will some day assert their freedom in the name of Almighty God." This is a marvelous prediction. Notice that it is not written "Immortals" but it is written "*mortals.*" How can a mortal assert anything at all when, as we have proven by the dream illustration, a mortal is a myth, a soul in a dream state?

The man on the couch need not assert that he is on the couch, for this is obvious and he knows it. But the mind that is dreaming itself on foreign streets, this mind wishes to return to his own home and room; this mind is tired and weary and would like rest on the comfortable couch.

The man on the couch does not need rest and repose for he has it, but this mind in the dream feels the need of this very thing; hence, since he feels the need, let him assert—in the dream—his freedom from those streets and from that country. Let him assert his freedom *in the name of the man on the couch.* And lo! the dream vanishes. There is only one presence,—the man on the couch.

Now the being of perpetual harmony does not

need immortal health and glory for he has it. But the mortal being, or the one in the dream of material existence, feels the need of this very thing, and since he it is who feels his need of health and harmony, let him assert—in the dream of material existence—his freedom from sickness, sin and trouble. Let him assert his freedom *in the name of Almighty God*. And lo! the dream of disease and discord vanishes. There is only one presence,—Almighty God, the one Being.

Thus while we seem to be in the dream of material existence and while we are called "mortals," we assert our freedom in the name of God, for what other name is there that shall deliver us? This is the name written in our foreheads, this is the name of our perfect being. Joyfully we believe it, we claim it, we accept it, we love it.

When the one dreaming himself on foreign land recognizes that he is all the while on the couch, he enters his abode of peace and rest.

And when "mortals" assert their freedom in the name of eternal Truth, they find their heritage of glory and immortality.

Treatment is the acceptance of our freedom as spiritual beings. A real being cannot be sick, and most certainly an unreal being cannot be sick. For one to know that he is real being, Spirit, is for him to experience a body that utters no complaints. This is what is meant by "the Spirit beareth witness with our spirit." (Romans 8:16).

When it is clear to us that our true convictions are founded upon Truth, we realize that actual Truth supports us, and that Truth is all that can ever control erring sense. Hence, as we establish Truth in our consciousness, we are assured of victory and we regain our sense of paradise.

Let sense awaken to spiritual interpretation of true being. Let beliefs in limitations, bondage, personality be set aside for higher views and perceptions. The awakening to the spiritual recognition and acceptance of self as Soul is the coming of Christ to the individual, revealing Paradise as a present reality.

As we advance in spiritual understanding, we perceive that right interpretation is the beginning of wisdom. Interpreting a spiritual being spiritually, one spontaneously rises to new heights, wherein is disclosed to him the co-existence of Soul and universe, and their unfallen spiritual perfection.

Absolute Science reveals that Omnipotence actually enthroned in every heart, must be individually acknowledged and demonstrated. Recognizing and claiming self as Christ, God, sense is lifted to a higher basis, opening prison doors and letting in the light of glory. Lifted to the inspired consciousness of *Soul and body as one*, perfect, immaculate all-harmonious, brings Paradise on earth.

Our ascension from faith to power, from sense to glory, from cross to crown constitutes our Paradise. To the awakened consciousness sense has left the cradle of mistification and bondage for the crown of irresistible glory. The crown that no man taketh from us is *spiritual understanding*, set with the dazzling jewels of transcending love, light and power.

The eternal verities of Being, apprehended, claimed and practiced, light our pathway with victory, delivering to us emancipation from the false sense of sin, sickness, and death and revealing to us the glories and splendors of supernal existence.

Let us relinquish the cross testifying to trial and tribulation and accept the crown of enlightened understanding. Here we rest in the peace of conscious strength and power, and in the practical demonstration of "Christ in you the hope of glory."

The recognition of the self as Soul, Spirit, Life, Truth, Love, strikes the note of universal freedom, gently delivering all from erring sense and lifting them to the consciousness of life as forever changeless, eternal, glowing and harmonious.

Paradise is the discovery, the acceptance and the experience of our actual entity.

If there is no selfhood apart from God then *selfhood is God*. If there is no being separate from the One then *all being is the One*. If body is the expression of Life, Truth and Love then *body is perfect, ideal and glorious*.

The *preaching of the gospel* is the *presentation* of the changeless continuance of good; of the ever-presence of reality, glory, happiness, harmony, health on earth as in heaven.

The *healing of the sick* is the *utilization* and *practice* of right interpretation and insight, the delivery to the individual of his reality, his perfection, his glory.

The *casting out of demons* is the *forsaking* of false beliefs, the *relinquishing* of erring notions. We do not give up the body, we give up the false idea of the body. We do not give up the universe, we give up the false idea of the universe. We do not give up pleasures, companionships, activities, we give up false ideas of pleasures, companionships, activities.

The *raising of the dead* is the experiencing of uninterrupted peace, harmony and immortality.

With spiritual vision we behold Paradise as a reality here and now, an experience of heavenly peace, glory, harmony, delight. The preaching of the Kingdom of paradise on earth is the presentation of the golden Message: *Be still, and know that I am God.*

Truth brings its own peace and harmony. Truth delivers its own joy, inspiration and uplift. Truth can say unto darkened sense, You cannot come into my presence without acknowledging Me as the *one* and *only* power and reality.

"*And this is life eternal that they might know thee, the only true God.*" This is life eternal that we shall recognize and know our reality and identity as the only true God.

Let one vision, think and act from the standpoint of his Lordship. If one feels that he needs quickening and illumination, that he needs the fire of Spirit, let him read the Bible and such books as contain spiritual quickening. Light kindles light, and a lighted consciousness transmits illumination.

Claiming our identity with Spirit only, we begin to have right ideas and right visions. *"This sickness is for the glory of God,"* said Jesus with loving assurance. Rising to the consciousness of our full dominion of Spirit we glorify our God-being. Healing is not actually healing, resurrecting is not actually resurrecting. *God is changeless reality.* We are changeless reality. Opening our vision to this supernal verity, we transcend the human steps called healing, overcoming, progressing; we see face to face; we discover that we have *already* arrived, and that we are perfect *without the process of progression.*

This is the Science of Ascension, the Science of ascending above earthly states and *conceptions*. This is the Science of laborless acceptance and experience.

When one places himself under the action of his thought and its consequences, he hinders his advancement; but when one places himself *above* his thoughts, spontaneously he rises to greater heights.

The notion that a thought or a thing can exist independently of Principle is false, and this falsity is vanquished by the realization and consciousness of the true facts of being. Transcending the *belief* in limitation and bondage, the so-called limitation and bondage disappears.

We acknowledge ourselves as free, unfettered, flawless, triumphant. We acknowledge our universe as heavenly, glorious, radiant, supernal. To know that we ourselves are Truth triumphant strikes the keynote of higher claims. As there is a strength above the strength of the body and a power above the power of the mentality so is there a Way above the way of progression.

This way is the Science of Ascension, the Science of recognizing a perfect universe and perfect being *here* and *now*. This sublime consciousness bridges over the periods called birth, age and death, and one finds himself in Heaven, the only universe, and in the full consciousness of his immortality and glory.

I am the flame, I am the inspiration, I am the finished wholeness and completion. I am awake, alive, for evermore. Nothing can separate me from being God—"neither death, nor life, nor powers, nor things present, nor things to come."

Insight accepts the kingdom of Heaven on earth. Insight reports that we are all one life, substance, being. Insight lifts us to the Mount and discloses to us our real identity. Insight delivers the ultimate understanding, the *ascension,* which is the *experience* of supernal glory, harmony and immortality.

Looking *up*, we perceive that nothing was impossible with Jesus, that nothing is impossible with us. Exalted vision discloses that there is no departure nor lapse from perfection and no return to perfection; but always, everywhere, there is one entity and one expression. As in the night one sees glowing stars, so right now, no matter how dark may seem your pathway, look up and behold this golden Light before you. *Accept* your real identity and *love* this identity. Your triumph and your redemption are, here, already established, waiting your acceptance.

One wakens from a dream by knowing that *he* is not in the dream. We are the dreamless, the ageless, the deathless reality. We are the all-conquering, the self-existing, the un-changeable Christ.

CHAPTER VII.

Roll Away the Stone

SUPPOSE one desiring a certain precious and marvelous jewel searches and looks everywhere, but all in vain. The gem of his dream cannot be found.

Finally, one day a friend comes into his presence presenting him with a handsome velvet box. "In this box," says the friend, "you will find that for which you have long been searching. Here is the jewel of your heart. Take it for it is yours."

Now, what is the first thing that happens to this individual? It is this. His mind is at peace. He stops longing and wondering for he is at rest. He does not hasten to open the box, in fact, he rather delights in keeping it unopened for the moment, for behold, it is here; that which he has desired has at last come to pass.

Perhaps some one now reading these lines has problems, fears, troubles. Let this Message—*Science of Ascension*—be the precious Jewel, the priceless Treasure delivered into your hand.

There need now be no hurry about the overthrow of sin, sickness and limitation. You can now relax and be at peace, for to the heart has come the Light and Truth, and this Light and Truth means freedom, deliverance. This Truth means laborless emancipation from a sense that is material to a sense that is divine; from a mind that is darkened to a mind that is lighted; from experience that is discordant to experience that is joyous.

The Jewel is here. The mystery is unveiled. Now one sees the Way, one feels the joy, one receives the glory that Infinite Consciousness has prepared for those who arise and accept the way to that heavenly City and that perfect Land which in truth was never left. And into his experience comes a new heaven and a new earth, for former beliefs have passed away.

By virtue of the fact that we have abolished the belief that we are human and have accepted the understanding that we are Spirit, we are prepared to accept the glories of Ascension. By virtue of the fact that we are God-being, we *cannot* be sick and we *cannot die*. Our eyes now see and our ears now hear the wonderful things that are prepared for those who accept this glorious Vision.

Often it is asked why it is that some students apprehend and accept advanced ideas of Truth readily and easily; others apparently equally as eager and earnest do not accept the presentation but instead hold tenaciously to differing views and concepts.

The process of individual acceptance may be made clear by the following illustration. Suppose that a party of friends enter a new and beautifully furnished residence to examine its style, furniture, art, etc. In this party are an electrician, an artist, a musician, as well as children of varying ages.

They all enter this spacious and luxuriously furnished home. Do you see the musician giving his attention first of all to the tapestries, or to the floors, or the decorations of the ceiling? Indeed not. He finds the grand piano and for the time this absorbs his whole-attention. And the artist, —is he, too, stationed at the piano? Why, already he is wandering from room to room, engrossed with the etchings and paintings. The electrician examines the latest style of electric fixtures and is interested in the radio. The children amuse themselves with games and books; each adult seeks that which particularly captures his attention.

Now everything about this group of people is just as it should be at that moment, is it not?

Each one is following a certain mental inclination and culture and each one is finding pleasure and satisfaction at his particular point of attention.

It is quite like this with the great numbers of people who study the Bible and who study metaphysical works and messages. We find books, written by highly specialized minds, setting forth verses from the Bible to prove that Jesus was the son of man. On the same shelf with these books are others, written by equally respected minds, setting forth verses from the same Bible to prove that Jesus was the Son of God and actually God Himself. Year after year, century after century, new books of such character are being published.

It is like this when it comes to the study of metaphysical Science. It seems that from the same text book variously different ideas are received and promulgated. It simply means that one expresses himself according to his individual state of consciousness.

The child pursues life in a different direction

from the adult and each one absorbs from books and teachings that which corresponds to his present view of life and being. This is the reason why one can seemingly find in the Bible whatever will support *his* belief, no matter which side of the message he had adopted as his viewpoint. The Bible furnishes this paradox.

Jesus stated: "All power is given unto me in heaven and in earth"; yet, "Of mine own self I can do nothing." Another Biblical paradox: "The flesh profiteth nothing"—(*St. John* 6:63). "Flesh cannot inherit the Kingdom of God"—(1 *Cor.* 15:50); yet, "All flesh shall see the salvation of God"—(*St. Luke* 3:6). "That the life also of Jesus might be made manifest in our mortal flesh"—(2 *Cor.* 4:11). Another: "I form the light, and create darkness: I make peace, and create evil: I the Lord do all these things:—(*Is.* 45:7) yet, "God is light, and in him is no darkness at all"—(1*John* 1:5). "Thou are of purer eyes than to behold evil."—(*Hab.* 1:13).

The one of Insight is not dismayed by these seeing contradictions. Climbing the ladder of life, we choose what we shall see and believe. But there comes a time when we no longer choose, no longer separate, no longer adopt certain specific forms of beliefs, for now the paradox is plain to us, *we see on all sides and we reconcile all as one.*

We can now understand another's view no matter where he stands upon the ladder; also we can show him the next step ahead. To one of exalted vision all views blend into one great Reality, and at last one can say understandingly, *There is no evil.*

A child has the right to childhood and one in his study of life has a perfect right to think and act according to his vision. Indeed, what else can he do? Therefore, during the transitional period wherein one is choosing, selecting, balancing, arguing, separating and dividing, he acts according to his unfolding vision. He is seeing two factors, two sides to life, and he is choosing between them.

But when he has reached a certain peak of vision, perhaps slowly, perhaps swiftly, he perceives the paradox and he exclaims with the prophet, *"The darkness and the light are both alike."* From then on, he commences to perceive *oneness.* Wherever he looks, whatever he reads, in the office, in the home, on the screen, in the stars, lo, everything speaks to him of the *One* life, the *One* being, the *One* expression.

He sees now why it is that over the world is heard a word echoing from the superplane,—the word *Co-operation.* Does this not mean oneness, agreement, unity? Certainly it does. Down through the ages it has been eternally sounding. *"Let there be light!"* Multitudes are hearing as they never heard before and earnest and eager attention is focussed on peace, on harmony, on service, on love, on oneness.

"That which hath been is now; and that which

is to be hath already been"—(*Ecc.* 3:15). Every good thing that seems coming *to us* is already here. It is coming to individual recognition, that is all. It is being apprehended by individual consciousness. In reality, it has been from Eternity but now it is appearing to us, individually. This is the way in which "Creation" is finished, yet creation is constantly and eternally appearing to individual recognition.

With the dawning in consciousness of this view of oneness and indivisibility, one gently rises from a mortal, limited state of thinking to a free, immortal state of understanding. With this heavenly Vision there appears the new earth, for always corresponding expression accompanies ascending states of consciousness.

Verily, O Glorious Reality, Thy Kingdom is coming—*is here*—on earth as it is in Heaven.

Swiftly comes the end of darkness when light arrives. Swiftly over all the face of the earth comes the end of separation, division, opposition, ignorance,—for the Light of Reality is here. Illumination consumes all misunderstanding and the King of Love and Glory is enthroned in hearts, in social groups, in nations.

Day by day, the whole world is echoing back the Song of Angels:

"Glory to God in the highest and on earth peace, good will toward men."—(*St. Luke* 2:14)

Of what advantage is it to have a Selfhood that is God, almighty, unlimited, all-powerful, all-glorious if we do not let this One *live* in us, if we do not let this One *shine* in us, if we do not let this One *act* in us?

To realize freedom, authority, let us accept and practice the One Presence as ALL. In this way, that which has seemed false in our minds will be transcended, swallowed up by the good in our own true Nature.

As we perceive the allness of the One and the

oneness of the ALL, we can say, "Heaven is here, the desert blossoms as the rose, the lion and the lamb express the same being."

Ever it is I, the divine Mind, the Jesus Christ Self, which speaketh, saying, "*I am whole, I am perfect, I am wonderful, I am glorious, I am victorious, I am all and besides Me there is no other Authority.*"

Always there is a way of escape because of the mental nature of limitation. For example: A caterpillar cannot fly, but suppose he should wish that he might fly, of what avail would his wish be, since it is not the nature of the caterpillar to fly? There is a path, however, a way for him, unseen by reason. There is a way of deliverance. Let that entity put on (accept) the butterfly; then he can fly.

Now, the human being wishes to be perfect, to be free, to be well and divine. But it is not in the nature of a material being to be perfect, to be glorious, to be free and divine. Yet there is a solution, there is a way of fulfillment. The Way is that of Absolute Science.

Let the so-called mortal put off the state of false belief for the state of understanding. Let him emerge from material belief into spiritual ascension,—"from matter into Spirit,"—then automatically he is glorious, he is divine, he is free.

A butterfly need not crawl. *Neither need nor can an Immortal being function in sickness, sin and death.* Behold the Light. Behold the Way. Behold the Science of Ascension.

The God to whom we look, to whom we turn for deliverance, is verily our own true Being. The God who healeth and redeemeth and saveth is verily the Self of Jesus, the Self of You, the Self of Me, the one and only Self,—one God, one Totality.

It has been stated that we must translate the universe back into Spirit, that we must interpret spiritual things *spiritually*. For instance, we are to perceive that *we* are the divine Mind and that *we* manifest all which comprises the infinitude of Truth.

Jesus, while in human form, demonstrated the spiritual revelation of atonement, resurrection and ascension. As life is spiritually interpreted, material sense is put off for *spiritual Science*. This transition from lower or human sense of life to a new and higher sense, presents the way of fulfillment through earthly development. Jesus' nativity being a spiritual sense of a spiritual world, naturally his mission was to interpret the spiritual universe spiritually.

Inspiration is the light which illumines the darkness and reveals to us that like Jesus, *our* nativity is Spirit, Soul. In the dark hour let this inspiration shine for it is *inspiration* which individualizes infinite power, sweeping aside clouded sense as the breeze sweeps away mist. Inspiration proceeds from a consciousness which believes in *almighty* Truth, a consciousness which speaks *imperatively* from the basis of faith and understanding.

What "stone" or obstacle can withstand Omnipotence? When one has the living Fire, he fears nothing, for this living Flame is a law unto itself and is absolute Authority.

Whatever seems an obstacle in our path can be rolled away by insight and inspiration. The fire of courage, certainty, power, born of spiritual inspiration, is the flaming sword which turns every way to establish life as irresistible, triumphant, victorious and supreme.

The "new tongue" accompanies right interpretation. As one translates things into ideas, and ideas into Soul, he needs a higher expression to convey his advanced understanding and make practical the commands of Jesus.

Every advancing period delivers a higher and clearer interpretation of Being. As the vision of Truth becomes more fully interpreted and practiced, individuals will more clearly apprehend their original and absolute state of being. They will rise naturally and easily to the mount of Revelation, crowning earth with irresistible glory. Thought will soar above false beliefs to triumphant freedom and to the understanding and experience of ineffable love, light and glory.

Human experience gives us plenty of opportunity to express that spiritual dominion which was enthroned in us in the "beginning." Exercising this dominion one advances rapidly in spiritual vision and spiritual revelation.

The view *from the mountain peak* seems quite different from the view in the valley. Looking from the mount of spiritual vision one sees that the heavenly Kingdom has come to earth, that perfection, glory, harmony, immortality are established without beginning or ending and that this being is forever perfectly expressed and manifested.

Looking *from the valley* one perceives progress, advancement, regeneration; one perceives that seeds become plants, and that mortals become immortals through spiritualization and regeneration. From the mount of Vision one views the universe clearly and interprets it truly, while from the valley one looks through mistaken sense and interprets the perfect world imperfectly, untruly, materially.

Seeing the perfect universe through a veil or mist, one sees it by degrees, "step by step" ascending as the veil is lifted. For instance, when "healing" takes place, it appears as though the body had changed from sickness to health, and when one manifests life more abundantly it appears as though he were immortalizing the body.

The fact is, however, that no one cannot immortalize his body for the reason that this act has already been accomplished. The body is perfect now and this perfect body is recognized and understood when rightly viewed.

Roll away the stone of erring vision for "Behold, I make all things new."—(*Rev.* 24:5.) Into the mind there comes a new sense, a feeling of joyous inspiration and courage for now it is seen that while there is nothing to be done or outwardly accomplished *there is an inner viewpoint which shall be attained*. It is as this correct viewpoint is attained that we express the Truth in our daily experience.

There are not two beings, one spiritual and the other material, nor are there two worlds, one perfect and the other imperfect. Looking with clear vision one interprets all things spiritually, perfectly. Looking through mistaken sense one reports spiritual reality falsely, calling the spiritual being a material being and speaking of perfect universe as a material world.

Now that insight is here, we joyously accept it and we love life and we love all the activities of a perfect universe.

As one gains a clearer and clearer view of perfect Life and its perfect expression, it seems as though he were actually immortalizing and perfecting his body. He is perfecting his *viewpoint*, that is all; he is establishing *himself* on the Mountain Peak and is seeing life spiritually, instead of dwelling in the valley and interpreting life materially.

Proportionately as one widens his horizon does he more correctly view and interpret perfect, complete being and perfect, complete universe. No change ever takes place in perfect, established being or in perfect, established expression. Our prerogative is to know this sublime reality and to apprehend this fact of being.

It is clearly seen that Jesus while on earth and "in the flesh," viewed a perfect universe and that he continually called this Kingdom to the attention of those around him. He also saw perfect Expression as everpresent. His instantaneous "healings" prove this fact.

Now when one individual is perceiving life and its expressions from the mountain Peak and another individual is viewing life and its expression from the valley, their reports seem opposed to each other. The one on the Peak reports beauty, harmony, glory, perfection, while he in the valley reports discord, sickness, sin, bondage.

Let it be very clearly grasped and fixed in consciousness that the discord is not opposing the harmony, that sickness is not the opposite of health, nor is bondage at war with freedom. It is a mistake to let mind accept the notion of separation, opposition, warfare, for nothing of this sort is present anywhere.

Let us adopt the new tongue, revising our vocabulary and striking out words which do not harmonize to the divine viewpoint. Why waste time and glory in discussing what isn't true? Why not hasten to the marriage feast already prepared, and eat and drink with our risen Lord? In proportion as one rises above mistaken sense and its viewpoint, he finds himself on the mountain Peak, understanding that the universe is *one,* and that whether one visions from the Peak or from the valley, what he sees is altogether a matter of consciousness.

Death is not the opposite of life, nor is evil the opposite of good, for the simple reason that one is *ever* present while the other is always illusion. If you enter a dimly lighted room and mistake a pedestal for an intruder would it not be practicing absurdity to declare the intruder the opposite of the pedestal?

In Omnipresence there are no opposites. This is right vision. This is the view beheld from the mountain Top. Never does the material expression contradict the spiritual reality; never does earth contradict heaven. Nothing can contradict Reality, for Reality is *all,* and Reality is *forever established.*

One ceases to mention "materiality" and "evil" when he apprehends and accepts completeness and uninterrupted fulness as *one* Presence now and here. Using the new tongue, erring expressions drop away naturally and without taking thought.

"We shall see him as he is" (1 *John* 3:2). It is an established certainty that we shall perceive perfect being and perfect universe as they are; that drinking of the living Waters we shall see face to face.

As mistaken sense fades out, one perceives reality more clearly. Misinterpreting this process of vision, however, one erringly speaks of reality as physical healing and physical improvement. It should be known that we do not restore the body; instead, we restore the *sense* of it; we restore the point of vision. This is accomplished by calmly and trustingly declaring that good is ever-present, that there are no opposites, that one Presence and one Experience are forever here and with us.

Every living thing enjoys freedom. Birds and animals and high souled men love great forests and unwalled spaces. All living things delight in freedom because Life itself is freedom. All living things cling to life. No matter how many years one has been in this world, even at the end he wishes to remain in it, to stay a little longer, to prolong the time with loved ones. Why is that? Because Soul cannot consider destruction. Life knows no such thing as death. Life and its individual activity *cannot* be separated.

We give ourselves to the One and there remains no sense of personality, no notion of separation. It is because the One is our Life and is our Heart that we can never be entirely satisfied with the joys and pleasures of this world. Do we not see men continually searching after happiness, always eager to have greater abundance, never quite satisfied, but always seeking just a little further ahead? Now, one may believe that he is seeking pleasure in material things, greater abundance of wealth, nearer and dearer companionships, but all the while it is Truth that he is seeking. He is seeking his heart, his treasure, *himself*.

Now, in one language this is called Evolution and in another language is called Progress; but rising above languages we see that one shall find himself, that one shall meet his own glory and shall know his own divinity. One will never be satisfied with less than ALL because his nature is the unlimited, the eternal, the infinite. It may seem to him that he seeks companionship, wealth, amusement, but even though he may know it not, he seeks the Unchangeable; he seeks the Unlimited, the Infinite, the Eternal.

Seeking his perfection, his Reality, he will never desist until he finds it,—until he comes face to face with his own glory. *"As for me, I shall be satisfied when I awake with Thy likeness."* (*Ps.* 17:15).

We naturally love all things beautiful, lovely, desirable, not really for things themselves as one may believe, but for the Self. The Self is beauty and so loves beauty. We desire wealth, unlimited abundance of all things not for the sake of wealth itself, that we may accumulate or hoard it, but for the Self. The Self is the eternal wealth of joy and satisfaction.

We love people, friends, companions, relatives not that we may attach ourselves to them, but we love them because we see in them the Self. The Self knows that It is Universal and Omnipresent and so constantly and continually seeks to express and embody itself. The Source of all joy, peace, satisfaction, glory is Us, the Self.

We are here for a greater destiny than to function in time and space. There is Something in us which urges us ever up and on, which promises that we shall be conscious of our *Omnipresence* and be instantly wherever we wish to be; that we shall become conscious of our *Omniscience* and have instantly revealed to us any particular knowledge that we may desire at the moment; that we shall be conscious of our *Omnip-*

otence and merely speak the Word and it shall come to pass; that we shall become conscious of our *Immortality* and live forever.

The Christ eternally breathes upon us the Message of our everlasting Glory, Wonder, Power Majesty and Immortality.

If we feel burdened by matter and mind, by belief in the hardness of human problems, we rise up and sing; we take our hymn book and raise our voice in song and praise. One cannot sing long without the feeling that he is lifted *above* his problem. Song inspires and lifts up the mind so that seeming troubles begin to manifest less of proportion, less of weight, and soon they appear smaller and farther away.

We sing until we FEEL the Answer within us, feel the warmth and the glory of peace and power. Throughout the Bible one may find that there are many examples of quick deliverance and emancipation from erring belief through song and praise.

"Roll away the stone!" Sing and praise Life for its wonderful freshness and ever-restoring fairness and loveliness. Praise Intelligence for Its omnipotence and dominion. Praise Love for Its ever-flowing affection and forgiveness. Praise Truth for Its outpouring abundance and its wealth of living ideas. Open the heart and let it rejoice in song; let it come into its own,— the Kingdom of supernal delight.

Song brings a quickening, a melting down of false beliefs in the mind, a breaking away of clouds, a rending of the tomb of ignorance. Roll ye away the stone!

Whatever seems a tomb enclosing one in the delusion of darkness and night, his song can roll the stone away. Jesus, coming to the tomb of his friend, issued the order, *Roll away the stone!* Now, he who found it possible to reproduce the presence of Lazarus, so that he walked forth in triumphant glory, could certainly have caused the stone to roll away without assistance,—

other than the Authority of the Word alone.

Jesus saw something, however, that these people could now do for themselves, something that would symbolize the rolling away of a stone of much greater importance. In the midst of every individual is this all-knowing Power which can roll away the stone or seeming obstacle.

Those who say that they have never felt the Presence, heard the Voice, nor seen the Light, have nevertheless read the words, *"Believe in Me."* Begin at once to believe in this omnipresent Christ, and begin at once to *accept* this Christ *as your own Self*. Accepting, believing, watching, praising, one reaches Understanding which is able to do all things for him.

We are conscious of our hands and feet, *why should we not be conscious of our Life and Soul?*

Now this living Soul has been called the Christ, the Superconscious Mind, the Father, and many other terms. But the underlying meaning is the same,—*it is one Being, it is one Reality.*

Learn the Science of Ascension and be *free*. Through the understanding and practice of this Science you will control error with Truth, sense with Soul, and belief with Understanding.

As one sees that he himself is the Trinity, that he himself is the Light and the Way, *he becomes fearless and free.*

How can one help but receive that which is his very own, that which ever remains awaiting his recognition and acceptance? From beginning to end, from eternity to eternity he is destined to come into realization that the Kingdom of God is his and that his actual being is the One.

Ascension is the *exercise* of one's inherent Glory. Ascension is the *drinking* of living Water and the *partaking* of heavenly Bread.

It is predestined from eternity, that at some time in the experience of every individual, false sense will be found unreal and untrue, and true Consciousness will be found complete and ever-present.

Revelation brings all things to our remembrance, transcending the evidence of the material senses and translating sense and language back into their original tongue and substance.

Let us not be selfish with this glorious Understanding and Light but let us give it freely to the universe. Let us rejoice to see the spreading of Truth no matter who speaks it nor what avenue opens for its expression. When we can look upon everyone as ourself, blessing all efforts to bring the Kingdom of heaven on earth, then we are *practicing* our vision and are beholding the divine Science which has rolled away the stone from the sepulchre of our Lord.

Let us say, "All the good I ever thought, all the good I ever said or did, this good was not mine but was Thine. Let the universe take it. Let all who will take it, for what is Thine is universal, having no attachment, having no will but the will of universal love and brotherhood."

So shall we receive freely even as we give freely. And the good that we do, the wisdom that we speak, will be so wonderful, so great in light and glory, that our personal self will be entirely lost sight of and the impersonal and universal Christ will reign supreme. Then indeed are we glorified. Then indeed are we prepared to behold the Creation which is perfect and good and *which can be seen face to face.*

Discovering the power of Insight to break the dream of false sense, we spiritualize thought and action, demonstrating the unreality of sin, sickness and discord.

A material sense of life is all that has to be relinquished and this action takes place automatically as one perceives and accepts his actual Being and his actual heritage. Material sense yields to the Science of Ascension in proportion as one learns and practices the radiance of his free, flawless and triumphant Self.

The Science of Reality wipes away tears, lifts

off shackles and delivers Glory, Power, Insight and Triumph.

Sickness, sin, limitation, bondage, exist only as *false sense*, and as this darkened sense is controlled with the light of spiritual Perception and Understanding, such limitation and bondage cease and one finds himself free, unfettered and harmonious.

The power of light over darkness is universally accepted and utilized. Likewise the "new tongue," explaining the power of enlightened spiritual sense over mistaken deluded belief, is rapidly coming into a wider recognition and acceptance.

The foundation of spiritual healing is Truth. Insight, Understanding. As one attains a mind in harmony with Truth, he *laborlessly* experiences a body governed and controlled by harmony.

Every step we take spiritually places us more firmly and surely in the realm of conscious joy, glory and happiness. The emancipation of our bodies from sickness, our minds from fear, and our lives from discord, follows the perception, understanding and acceptance of our being as the Unlimited, Adorable, and Eternal.

In the Science of Omnipotence there is no lo, here! or lo, there! but steadily, firmly, we keep our mind on the fact that there is but *one* Substance, *one* Power, *one* Life and *one* Being.

When spiritual perception reaches Truth then error is subdued and it disappears. The human mind, advancing above itself toward sublime Reality, relinquishes the mistaken and transcient view for spiritual perception and divine consciousness.

Thus as mind accepts spiritual understanding, it rises above all falsity, and the divine Consciousness is found to be the only Mind, Intelligence and Actuality. Then appear a new heaven and a new earth and former views and things will have passed away.

Sin, sickness, death, are unsustained by Truth and will disappear and be swallowed up in spiritual Truth and Reality,—in Victory, Ascension and Triumph.

Revelation and illumination, transmitted by spiritual Consciousness, correct erring sense and erring belief, transforming earth with triumphal glory.

Because the One is all being, and all being is the One, a realization of this fact will deliver us from evil and will open our vision to behold the spiritual phenomena of divine Reality.

Consciousness, held in a false sense of existence, will be uplifted, purified and elevated, either by *ascension* or by the *progressive human steps*, until all come into the knowledge of Reality and rise superior to limited sense and existence.

Accept the joys and glories of your real being. True understanding will roll away the stone and will open for you the door to supernal delights.

You can achieve all good, all joy and all happiness. See first the understanding of spiritual Reality, (the Kingdom of heaven), then the abundance of infinite glories, pleasures, and harmonies, will be showered upon you.

As the heart accepts the sublime message that individual being is Being individualized, under the law of Love—the law of the Christ presence, consciousness is then released from its fears and darkness, and spontaneously it rises to behold the spotless glory of spiritual being, spiritual body, and spiritual universe.

It has been said that all spiritual teaching in this world may be rightly grouped under three headings. The first heading is: I AM HIS. Here God is thought of in the third person. One talks *about* God. One sings *about* God. One says, "*I am His*" as though God were a great way off.

The second group or heading is this: "I AM THINE." God is now being brought closer to the individual. God is not spoken of or about, but

God is spoken *to*. God now becomes nearer and nearer. God hears and answers prayer.

In the third position the veil of duality is torn completely away. *Oneness* now holds the vision, and the cry is: "I AM THOU." Now "mine" and "Thine" are the same. *The One* is recognized, acknowledged and accepted as *all*.

Thus shall we not all find that, one after another, we have taken just these three positions in our seeming journey from sense to Soul? *I am His! I am Thine! I am Thou!*

"Arise, shine; thy light is come;
The glory of the Lord is upon thee."

FINIS